PRAISE FOR *ELOQUENT JAVASCRIPT*

"A concise and balanced mix of principles and pragmatics. I loved the tutorial-style game-like program development. This book rekindled my earliest joys of programming. Plus, JavaScript!"
—BRENDAN EICH, CREATOR OF JAVASCRIPT

"I became a better architect, author, mentor, and developer because of this book."
—ANGUS CROLL, TWITTER DEVELOPER

"If you decide to purchase only one JavaScript book, that book should be Marijn Haverbeke's *Eloquent JavaScript*."
—JOEY deVILLA, GLOBAL NERDY

"One of the greatest texts for not just learning JavaScript but for learning modern programming in general as told through JavaScript. This is the book I give out when people ask me how to learn proper JavaScript."
—CHRIS WILLIAMS, ORGANIZER OF JSCONF US

"One of the best JavaScript books I've read."
—REY BANGO, JQUERY TEAM MEMBER AND CLIENT-WEB COMMUNITY PROGRAM MANAGER AT MICROSOFT

"This book is a really good guide to JavaScript; but even more than that, this book is a great guide to programming."
—BEN NADEL, CHIEF SOFTWARE ENGINEER AT EPICENTER CONSULTING

"A fantastic book."
—DESIGN SHACK

"*Eloquent JavaScript* does a good job of detailing the fundamentals and explaining concepts like the stack and the environment. This attention to detail is what sets the book apart from other JavaScript books."
—DESIGNORATI

"A great book if you're learning JavaScript."
—CRAIG BUCKLER, OPTIMALWORKS WEB DESIGN

Eloquent JavaScript

A Modern Introduction to Programming

Marijn Haverbeke

no starch
press

Printed on demand in the USA

ISBN-10: 1-59327-282-0
ISBN-13: 978-1-59327-282-1

Publisher: William Pollock
Production Editor: Serena Yang
Cover and Interior Design: Octopod Studios
Developmental Editor: Keith Fancher
Technical Reviewer: Patrick Corcoran
Copyeditor: Kim Wimpsett
Compositor: Serena Yang
Proofreader: Nancy Sixsmith

For information on distribution, translations, or bulk sales, please contact No Starch Press, Inc. directly:

No Starch Press, Inc.
245 8th Street, San Francisco, CA 94103
phone: 415.863.9900; fax: 415.863.9950; info@nostarch.com; www.nostarch.com

Library of Congress Cataloging-in-Publication Data

```
Haverbeke, Marijn.
  Eloquent JavaScript: a modern introduction to programming / by Marijn Haverbeke.
       p. cm.
  Includes index.
  ISBN-13: 978-1-59327-282-1
  ISBN-10: 1-59327-282-0
  1.  JavaScript (Computer program language)  I. Title.
  QA76.73.J39H38 2009
  005.13'3-dc22
                                  2010032246
```

To little Lotte.

BRIEF CONTENTS

CONTENTS IN DETAIL

2
FUNCTIONS   29

3
DATA STRUCTURES: OBJECTS AND ARRAYS   41

4
ERROR HANDLING 63

5
FUNCTIONAL PROGRAMMING 71

6
OBJECT-ORIENTED PROGRAMMING 93

7
MODULARITY

129

11
BROWSER EVENTS

12
HTTP REQUESTS

INDEX

INTRODUCTION

Back in the 1970s, when personal computers were first introduced, most of them came equipped with a simple programming language—usually a variant of BASIC—and interaction with the computer required use of this language. This meant that, for those of us to whom technological tinkering came naturally, going from simple computer use to programming was easy.

These days, with computers being many times more powerful and cheaper than in the 1970s, software interfaces tend to present a slick graphics interface manipulated with the mouse, rather than a language. This has made computers much more accessible and, on the whole, is a big improvement. However, it has also put up a barrier between the computer user and the world of programming—hobbyists have to actively *find* themselves a programming environment rather than having one available as soon as the computer starts.

Under the covers, our computer systems are still pervaded by various programming languages. Most of these languages are much more advanced than the BASIC dialects in those early personal computers. For example, the JavaScript language, the subject of this book, exists in every mainstream web browser.

On Programming

> I do not enlighten those who are not eager to learn, nor arouse those who are not anxious to give an explanation themselves. If I have presented one corner of the square and they cannot come back to me with the other three, I should not go over the points again.
> —Confucius

Besides explaining JavaScript, this book tries to be an introduction to the basic principles of programming. Programming, it turns out, is hard. The fundamental rules are typically simple and clear—but programs, while built on top of these basic rules, tend to become complex enough to introduce their own rules and complexity. Because of this, programming is rarely simple or predictable. As Donald Knuth, who is something of a founding father of the field, says, it is an *art* rather than a science.

To get something out of this book, more than just passive reading is required. Try to stay sharp, make an effort to understand the example code, and only continue when you are reasonably sure you understand the material that came before.

> The computer programmer is a creator of universes for which he alone is responsible. Universes of virtually unlimited complexity can be created in the form of computer programs.
> —Joseph Weizenbaum, *Computer Power and Human Reason*

A program is many things. It is a piece of text typed by a programmer, it is the directing force that makes the computer do what it does, it is data in the computer's memory, yet it controls the actions performed on this same memory. Analogies that try to compare programs to objects we are familiar with tend to fall short, but a superficially fitting one is that of a machine. The gears of a mechanical watch fit together ingeniously, and if the watchmaker was any good, it will accurately show the time for many years. The elements of a program fit together in a similar way, and if programmers know what they are doing, their program will run without crashing.

A computer is a machine built to act as a host for these immaterial machines. Computers themselves can only do stupidly straightforward things. The reason they are so useful is that they do these things at an incredibly high speed. A program can ingeniously combine enormous numbers of these simple actions in order to do very complicated things.

To some of us, writing computer programs is a fascinating game. A program is a building of thought. It is costless to build, it is weightless, and it grows easily under our typing hands. If we are not careful, its size and complexity will grow out of control, confusing even the person who created it. This is the main problem of programming: keeping programs under control. When a program works, it is beautiful. The art of programming is the skill of controlling complexity. The great program is subdued, made simple in its complexity.

Today, many programmers believe that this complexity is best managed by using only a small set of well-understood techniques in their programs. They have composed strict rules (*best practices*) about the form programs should have, and the more zealous among them will denounce those who break these rules as *bad* programmers.

What hostility to the richness of programming—to try to reduce it to something straightforward and predictable and to place a taboo on all the weird and beautiful programs! The landscape of programming techniques is enormous, fascinating in its diversity, and still largely unexplored. It is certainly littered with traps and snares, luring the inexperienced programmer into all kinds of horrible mistakes, but that only means you should proceed with caution and keep your wits about you. As you learn, there will always be new challenges and new territory to explore. Programmers who refuse to keep exploring will surely stagnate, forget their joy, and lose the will to program (and become managers).

Why Language Matters

In the beginning, at the birth of computing, there were no programming languages. Programs looked something like this:

```
00110001 00000000 00000000
00110001 00000001 00000001
00110011 00000001 00000010
01010001 00001011 00000010
00100010 00000010 00001000
01000011 00000001 00000000
01000001 00000001 00000001
00010000 00000010 00000000
01100010 00000000 00000000
```

That is a program to add the numbers from 1 to 10 together and print out the result (1 + 2 + ... + 10 = 55). It could run on a very simple, hypothetical machine. To program early computers, it was necessary to set large arrays of switches in the right position, or punch holes in strips of cardboard and feed them to the computer. You can imagine how this was a tedious, error prone procedure. Even the writing of simple programs required much cleverness and discipline, and complex ones were nearly inconceivable.

Of course, manually entering these arcane patterns of *bits* (which is what the ones and zeros shown previously are generally called) did give the programmer a profound sense of being a mighty wizard. And that has to be worth something in terms of job satisfaction.

Each line of the program contains a single instruction. It could be written in English like this:

1. Store the number 0 in memory location 0.

2. Store the number 1 in memory location 1.

3. Store the value of memory location 1 in memory location 2.

4. Subtract the number 11 from the value in memory location 2.

5. If the value in memory location 2 is the number 0, continue with instruction 9.

6. Add the value of memory location 1 to memory location 0.

7. Add the number 1 to the value of memory location 1.

8. Continue with instruction 3.

9. Output the value of memory location 0.

Although that is more readable than the binary soup, it is still rather unpleasant. It might help to use names instead of numbers for the instructions and memory locations:

```
Set 'total' to 0
Set 'count' to 1
[loop]
 Set 'compare' to 'count'
 Subtract 11 from 'compare'
 If 'compare' is zero, continue at [end]
 Add 'count' to 'total'
 Add 1 to 'count'
 Continue at [loop]
[end]
 Output 'total'
```

At this point it is not too hard to see how the program works. Can you? The first two lines give two memory locations their starting values: total will be used to build up the result of the computation, and count keeps track of the number that we are currently looking at. The lines using compare are probably the weirdest ones. What the program wants to do is see whether count is equal to 11 in order to decide whether it can stop yet. Because the machine is rather primitive, it can only test whether a number is zero and make a decision (jump) based on that. So, it uses the memory location labeled compare to compute the value of count - 11 and makes a decision based on that value. The next two lines add the value of count to the result and increment count by 1 every time the program has decided that it is not 11 yet.

Here is the same program in JavaScript:

```
var total = 0, count = 1;
while (count <= 10) {
  total += count;
  count += 1;
}
print(total);
```

This gives us a few more improvements. Most importantly, there is no need to specify the way we want the program to jump back and forth any more. The magic word while takes care of that. It continues executing the lines below it as long as the condition it was given holds: count <= 10, which means "count is less than or equal to 10." We no longer have to create a temporary value and compare that to zero. This was an uninteresting detail, and the power of programming languages is that they take care of uninteresting details for us.

Finally, here is what the program could look like if we happened to have the convenient operations range and sum available, which respectively create a collection of numbers within a range and compute the sum of a collection of numbers:

```
print(sum(range(1, 10)));
```

The moral of this story, then, is that the same program can be expressed in long and short, unreadable and readable ways. The first version of the program was extremely obscure, while this last one is almost English: print the sum of the range of numbers from 1 to 10. (We will see in later chapters how to build things like sum and range.)

A good programming language helps the programmer by providing a more abstract means of expression. It hides uninteresting details, provides convenient building blocks (such as the while construct), and, most of the time, allows the programmer to add new building blocks (such as the sum and range operations).

What Is JavaScript?

JavaScript is the language that is, at the moment, mostly being used to do all kinds of clever (and sometimes annoying) things with pages on the World Wide Web. In recent years, the language has started to be used in other contexts as well—for example, the *node.js* framework, a way to write fast server-side programs in JavaScript, has recently been attracting a lot of attention. If you are interested in programming, JavaScript is definitely a useful language to learn. Even if you do not end up doing a lot of web programming, some of the programs I will show you in this book will stay with you, haunt you, and influence the programs you write in other languages.

There are those who will say *terrible* things about the JavaScript language. Many of these things are true. When I was required to write something in JavaScript for the first time, I quickly came to despise it—it would accept almost anything I typed but interpret it in a way that was completely different from what I meant. This had, admittedly, a lot to do with the fact that I did not have a clue what I was doing, but there is a real issue here: JavaScript is ridiculously liberal in what it allows. The idea behind this design was that it would make programming in JavaScript easier for beginners. In actuality, it mostly makes finding problems in your programs harder, because the system will not point them out to you.

However, the flexibility of the language is also an advantage. It leaves space for a lot of techniques that are impossible in more rigid languages, and, as we will see in later chapters, it can be used to overcome some of JavaScript's shortcomings. After learning it properly and working with it for a while, I have really learned to *like* this language.

Contrary to what the name suggests, JavaScript has very little to do with the programming language named Java. The similar name was inspired by marketing considerations, rather than good judgment. In 1995, when JavaScript was introduced by Netscape, the Java language was being heavily marketed and was gaining in popularity. Apparently, someone thought it a good idea to try to ride along on this success. Now we are stuck with the name.

Related to JavaScript is a thing called ECMAScript. When browsers other than Netscape started to support JavaScript, or something that resembled it, a document was written to describe precisely how a JavaScript system should work. The language described in this document is called ECMAScript, after the organization that standardized it. ECMAScript describes a general-purpose programming language and does not say anything about the integration of this language in a web browser.

There have been several "versions" of JavaScript. This book describes ECMAScript version 3, the first version that was (and is) widely supported by various different browsers. In the past years, there have been several initiatives to further evolve the language, but, at least for web programming, these extensions are useful only once they are widely supported by browsers, and it will take a while for browsers to catch up with such developments. Fortunately, newer versions of JavaScript will mostly be an extension of ECMAScript 3, so almost everything written in this book will continue to hold.

Trying Programs

When you want to run the code shown in this book and play with it, one possibility is to go to *http://eloquentjavascript.net/* and use the tools provided there.

Another approach is to simply create an HTML file containing the program and load it in your browser. For example, you could create a file called *test.html* with the following content:

```
<html><body><script type="text/javascript">

var total = 0, count = 1;
while (count <= 10) {
  total += count;
  count += 1;
}
document.write(total);

</script></body></html>
```

Later chapters will tell you a little more about HTML and the way a browser interprets it. Note that the operation print in the example has been replaced with document.write. We will see how to create the print function in Chapter 10.

Overview of This Book

The first three chapters will introduce the JavaScript language and teach you how to write grammatically correct JavaScript programs. They introduce control structures (such as the while word we saw in this introduction), functions (writing your own operations), and data structures. This will teach you enough to write simple programs.

Building on this basic understanding of programming, the next four chapters discuss more advanced techniques—things that should make you capable of writing more complicated programs without them turning into an incomprehensible mess. First, Chapter 4 discusses handling errors and unexpected situations. Then, Chapters 5 and 6 introduce two major approaches to abstraction: functional programming and object-oriented programming. Chapter 7 gives some pointers on how to keep your programs organized.

The remaining chapters focus less on theory and more on the tools that are available in a JavaScript environment. Chapter 8 introduces a sublanguage for text processing, and Chapters 9 to 12 describe the facilities available to a program when it is running inside a browser—teaching you how to manipulate web pages, react to user actions, and communicate with a web server.

Typographic Conventions

In this book, text written in a monospaced font should be understood to represent elements of programs—sometimes they are self-sufficient fragments, and sometimes they just refer to part of a nearby program. Programs (of which you have already seen a few), are written as follows:

```
function fac(n) {
  return n == 0 ? 1 : n * fac(n - 1);
}
```

Sometimes, in order to demonstrate what happens when certain expressions are evaluated, the expressions are written in bold, and the produced value is written below, with an arrow in front of it:

```
1 + 1
→ 2
```

1

BASIC JAVASCRIPT: VALUES, VARIABLES, AND CONTROL FLOW

Inside the computer's world, there is only data—that which is not data does not exist. All this data is in essence just sequences of bits and is thus fundamentally alike. Bits are any kinds of two-valued things, usually described as 0s and 1s. Inside the computer, they take forms like a high or low electrical charge, a strong or weak signal, or a shiny or dull spot on the surface of a CD.

Values

Though made of the same uniform stuff, every piece of data plays its own role. In a JavaScript system, most of this data is neatly separated into things called *values*. Every value has a type, which determines the kind of role it can play. There are six basic types of values: numbers, strings, Booleans, objects, functions, and undefined values.

To create a value, one must merely invoke its name. This is very convenient. You don't have to gather building material for your values or pay for them; you just call for one, and *woosh*, you have it. They are not created from thin air, of course. Every value has to be stored somewhere, and if you want to use a gigantic amount of them at the same time you might run out of computer memory. Fortunately, this is a problem only if you need them all simultaneously. As soon as you no longer use a value, it will dissipate, leaving behind only a few bits. These bits are recycled to make the next generation of values.

Numbers

Values of the *number* type are, as you might have guessed, numeric values. They are written as numbers usually are:

144

Put that into a program, and it will cause the number 144 to come into existence inside the computer. This is what 144 might look like in bits:

0100000001100010000000000000000000000000000000000000000000000000

If you were expecting something like 10010000 here (which is the integer representation of 144) . . . good call. It might actually be represented like that in some situations. But the standard describes JavaScript numbers as 64-bit floating-point values. This means they can also contain fractions and exponents.

But we won't go too deeply into binary representations here. The interesting thing, to us, is the practical repercussions they have for our numbers. For one thing, the fact that numbers are represented by a limited amount of bits means they have a limited precision. A set of 64 1/0 values can represent only 2^{64} different numbers. This is a lot, though, more than 10^{19} (a 1 with 19 zeroes).

Not all whole numbers below 10^{19} fit in a JavaScript number. For one, there are also negative numbers, so one of the bits has to be used to store the sign of the number. A bigger issue is that nonwhole numbers must also be represented. To do this, 11 bits are used to store the position of the decimal dot within the number.

That leaves 52 bits.[1] Any whole number less than 2^{52}, which is more than 10^{15}, will safely fit in a JavaScript number. In most cases, the numbers we are using stay well below that.

Fractional numbers are written by using a dot:

9.81

For very big or very small numbers, one can also use "scientific" notation by adding an e, followed by the exponent of the number:

---

[1] Actually, 53, because of a trick that can be used to get one bit for free. Look up the "IEEE 754" format if you are curious about the details.

```
2.998e8
```

That is $2.998 \times 10^8 = 299800000$.

Calculations with whole numbers (also called *integers*) that fit in 52 bits are guaranteed to always be precise. Unfortunately, calculations with fractional numbers are generally not. Like π (pi) cannot be precisely expressed by a finite amount of decimal digits, many numbers lose some precision when only 64 bits are available to store them. This is a shame, but it causes practical problems only in very specific situations. The important thing is to be aware of it and treat fractional digital numbers as approximations, not as precise values.

Arithmetic

The main thing to do with numbers is arithmetic. Arithmetic operations such as addition or multiplication take two number values and produce a new number from them. Here is what they look like in JavaScript:

```
100 + 4 * 11
```

The + and * symbols are called *operators*. The first stands for addition, and the second stands for multiplication. Putting an operator between two values will apply it to those values and produce a new value.

Does the example mean "add 4 and 100, and multiply the result by 11," or is the multiplication done before the adding? As you might have guessed, the multiplication happens first. But, as in mathematics, this can be changed by wrapping the addition in parentheses:

```
(100 + 4) * 11
```

For subtraction, there is the - operator, and division can be done with /. When operators appear together without parentheses, the order in which they are applied is determined by the *precedence* of the operators. The example show that multiplication comes before addition. / has the same precedence as *, and likewise for + and -. When multiple operators with the same precedence appear next to each other (as in 1 - 2 + 1), they are applied left to right.

These rules of precedence are not something you should worry about. When in doubt, just add parentheses.

There is one more arithmetic operator, which is possibly less familiar to you. The % symbol is used to represent the *modulo* operation. X modulo Y is the remainder of dividing X by Y. For example, 314 % 100 is 14, 10 % 3 is 1, and 144 % 12 is 0. Modulo's precedence is the same as that of multiplication and division.

Strings

The next data type is the *string*. Its use is not as evident from its name as with numbers, but it also fulfills a very basic role. Strings are used to represent text. (The name supposedly derives from the fact that it strings together a bunch of characters.) Strings are written by enclosing their content in quotes:

```
"Patch my boat with chewing gum."
'You ain\'t never seen a donkey fly!'
```

Both single and double quotes can be used to mark strings—as long as the quotes at the start and the end of the string match.

Almost anything can be put between quotes, and JavaScript will make a string value out of it. But a few characters are tricky. You can imagine how putting quotes between quotes might be hard. Newlines, the things you get when you press ENTER, can also not be put between quotes—the string has to stay on a single line.

To be able to have such characters in a string, the following trick is used: Whenever a backslash (\) is found inside quoted text, it indicates that the character after it has a special meaning. A quote that is preceded by a backslash will not end the string, but be part of it. When an n character occurs after a backslash, it is interpreted as a newline. Similarly, a t after a backslash means a tab character. Take the following string:

```
"This is the first line\nAnd this is the second"
```

The actual text contained is this:

```
This is the first line
And this is the second
```

There are, of course, situations where you want a backslash in a string to be just a backslash, not a special code. If two backslashes follow each other, they will collapse right into each other, and only one will be left in the resulting string value. This is how the string A newline character is written like "\n" can be written:

```
"A newline character is written like \"\\n\"."
```

Strings cannot be divided, multiplied, or subtracted. The + operator *can* be used on them. It does not add, but it concatenates; it glues two strings together. The following line will produce the string "concatenate":

```
"con" + "cat" + "e" + "nate"
```

There are more ways of manipulating strings, which we will discuss later.

Unary Operators

Not all operators are symbols; some are written as words. One example is the typeof operator, which produces a string value naming the type of the value you give it:

```
typeof 4.5
→ "number"
typeof "x"
→ "string"
```

The other operators we saw all operated on two values; typeof takes only one. Operators that use two values are called *binary* operators, while those that take one are called *unary* operators. The minus operator can be used both as a binary operator and a unary operator:

```
- (10 - 2)
→ -8
```

Boolean Values, Comparisons, and Boolean Logic

Next, we look at values of the *Boolean* type. There are only two of these: true and false. Here is one way to produce them:

```
3 > 2
→ true
3 < 2
→ false
```

I hope you have seen the > and < signs before. They mean, respectively, "is greater than" and "is less than." They are binary operators, and the result of applying them is a Boolean value that indicates whether they hold true in this case.

Strings can be compared in the same way:

```
"Aardvark" < "Zoroaster"
→ true
```

The way strings are ordered is more or less alphabetic: Uppercase letters are always "less" than lowercase ones, so "Z" < "a" is true, and nonalphabetic characters (!, @, and so on) are also included in the ordering. The actual way in which the comparison is done is based on the *Unicode* standard. This standard assigns a number to virtually every character one would ever need, including characters from Greek, Arabic, Japanese, Tamil, and so on. Having such numbers is practical for storing strings inside a computer—you can represent them as a sequence of numbers. When comparing strings, JavaScript goes over them from left to right, comparing the numeric codes of the characters one by one.

Other similar operators are >= ("is greater than or equal to"), <= ("is less than or equal to"), == ("is equal to"), and != ("is not equal to").

```
"Itchy" != "Scratchy"
→ true
```

There are also some operations that can be applied to Boolean values themselves. JavaScript supports three logical operators: *and*, *or*, and *not*. These can be used to "reason" about Booleans.

The && operator represents logical *and*. It is a binary operator, and its result is true only if both the values given to it are true.

```
true && false
→ false
true && true
→ true
```

|| is the logical *or*; it is true if either of the values given to it is true:

```
false || true
→ true
false || false
→ false
```

Not is written as an exclamation mark, !. It is a unary operator that flips the value given to it; !true produces false, and !false gives true.

When mixing these Boolean operators with arithmetic and other operators, it is not always obvious when parentheses are needed. In practice, one can usually get by with knowing that of the operators we have seen so far, || has the lowest precedence, then comes &&, then the comparison operators (>, ==, and so on), and then the rest. This has been chosen in such a way that, in typical situations, as few parentheses as possible are necessary.

Expressions and Statements

All the examples so far have used the language like you would use a pocket calculator: We made some values and then applied operators to them to get new values. Creating values like this is an essential part of every JavaScript program, but it is only a part. A piece of code that produces a value is called an *expression*. Every value that is written directly (such as 22 or "psychoanalysis") is an expression. An expression between parentheses is also an expression. And a binary operator applied to two expressions, or a unary operator applied to one, is also an expression. Using these rules, you can build up expressions of arbitrary size and complexity. (JavaScript actually has a few more ways of building expressions, which will be revealed when the time is ripe.)

There exists a unit that is bigger than an expression. It is called a *statement*. A program is built as a list of statements. Most statements end with a semicolon (;). The simplest kind of statement is an expression with a semicolon after it. This is a program:

```
1;
!false;
```

It is a useless program, though. An expression can be content to just produce a value, but a statement amounts to something only if it somehow changes the world. It could print something to the screen—that counts as changing the world—or it could change the internal state of the program in a way that will affect the statements that come after it. These changes are called *side effects*. The statements in the previous example just produce the values 1 and true and then immediately throw them away again. This leaves no impression on the world at all and is not a side effect.

In some cases, JavaScript allows you to omit the semicolon at the end of a statement. In other cases, it has to be there, or strange things will happen. The rules for when it can be safely omitted are complex and weird—the basic idea is that if a program is invalid but inserting a semicolon can make it valid, the program is treated as if the semicolon is there. In this book, every statement that needs a semicolon will always be terminated by one, and I strongly urge you to do the same in your own programs.

Variables

How does a program keep an internal state? How does it remember things? We have seen how to produce new values from old values, but this does not change the old values, and the new value has to be immediately used or it will dissipate again. To catch and hold values, JavaScript provides a thing called a *variable*.

```
var caught = 5 * 5;
```

A variable always has a name, and it can point at a value, holding on to it. The previous statement creates a variable called caught and uses it to grab hold of the number that is produced by multiplying 5 by 5.

After a variable has been defined, its name can be used as an expression that produces the value it holds. Here's an example:

```
var ten = 10;
ten * ten;
→ 100
```

The word var is used to create a new variable. After var, the name of the variable follows. Variable names can be almost every word, but they may not include spaces. Digits can also be part of variable names—catch22 is a valid name, for example—but the name must not start with a digit. The characters $ and _ can be used in names as if they were letters. So, for example, $_$ is a correct variable name.

If you want the new variable to immediately capture a value, which is often the case, the = operator can be used to give it the value of some expression.

When a variable points at a value, that does not mean it is tied to that value forever. At any time, the = operator can be used on existing variables to disconnect them from their current value and have them point to a new one:

```
caught;
→ 25
caught = 4 * 4;
caught;
→ 16;
```

You should imagine variables as tentacles, rather than boxes. They do not *contain* values; they *grasp* them—two variables can refer to the same value. Only the values that the program still has a hold on can be accessed by it. When you need to remember something, you grow a tentacle to hold on to it, or you reattach one of your existing tentacles to a new value.

For example, to remember the amount of dollars that Luigi still owes you, you create a variable for it. And then, when he pays back $35, you give this variable a new value.

```
var luigisDebt = 140;
luigisDebt = luigisDebt - 35;
luigisDebt;
→ 105
```

Keywords and Reserved Words

Note that names that have a special meaning, such as var, may not be used as variable names. These are called *keywords*. There are also a number of words that are "reserved for use" in future versions of JavaScript. These are also officially not allowed to be used as variable names, though some browsers do allow them. The full list is rather long:

```
abstract boolean break byte case catch char class const continue debugger
default delete do double else enum export extends false final finally float
for function goto if implements import in instanceof int interface long native
new null package private protected public return short static super switch
synchronized this throw throws transient true try typeof var void volatile
while with
```

Don't worry about memorizing these, but remember that this might be the problem when something does not work as expected. In my experience, char (to store a one-character string) and class are the most common names accidentally used.

The Environment

The collection of variables and their values that exist at a given time is called the *environment*. When a program starts up, this environment is not empty. It always contains a number of standard variables. When your browser loads a page, it creates a new environment and attaches these standard values to it. The variables created and modified by programs on that page survive until the browser goes to a new page.

Functions

A lot of the values provided by the standard environment have the type *function*. A function is a piece of program wrapped in a value. Generally, this piece of program does something useful, which can be invoked using the function value that contains it. In a browser environment, the variable alert, for example, holds a function that shows a little dialog box with a message. It is used like this:

```
alert("Good morning!");
```

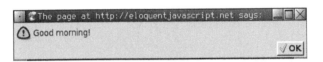

Executing the code in a function is called *invoking* or *applying* it. The notation for doing this uses parentheses. Every expression that produces a function value can be invoked by putting parentheses after it, though usually you will be directly referring to the variable that holds the function. The string value between the parentheses is given to the function, which uses it as the text to show in the dialog box. Values given to functions are called *arguments* (or sometimes *parameters*). alert needs only one of them, but other functions might need a different number or different types of arguments.

Showing a dialog box is a side effect. A lot of functions are useful because of the side effects they produce. It is also possible for a function to produce a value, in which case it does not need to have a side effect to be useful. For example, there is a function Math.max, which takes two arguments and gives back the biggest of the two:

```
Math.max(2, 4);
→ 4
```

When a function produces a value, it is said to *return* it. Because things that produce values are always expressions in JavaScript, function calls can be used as part of bigger expressions:

```
Math.min(2, 4) + 100;
→ 102
```

Chapter 2 discusses writing your own functions.

prompt and confirm

The standard environment provided by browsers contains a few more functions for popping up windows. You can ask the user an "OK"/"Cancel" question using confirm. This returns a Boolean: true if the user clicks OK and false if the user clicks Cancel.

```
confirm("Shall we, then?");
```

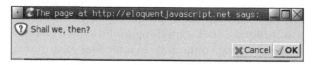

prompt can be used to ask an "open" question. The first argument is the question; the second one is the text that the user starts with. A line of text can be typed into the dialog window, and the function will return this as a string.

```
prompt("Tell me everything you know.", "...");
```

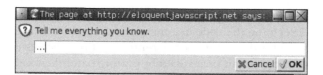

The print Function

As mentioned earlier, web browsers provide an alert function for showing a string in a little window. This can be useful when trying out code, but clicking away all those little windows can get on one's nerves. In this book we will pretend there exists a function named print, which writes out its arguments to some unspecified text output device. This will make it easier to write some of the examples. But note that the JavaScript environment provided by web browsers does not include this function.

For example, this will write out the letter X:

```
print("X");
```

Modifying the Environment

It is possible to give almost every variable in the environment a new value. This can be useful but also dangerous. If you give alert the value 8, it is no longer a function, and you won't be able to use it to show messages anymore. In Chapter 7, we will discuss how to protect against accidentally redefining variables.

Program Structure

One-line programs are not very interesting. When you put more than one statement into a program, the statements are executed, predictably enough, one at a time, from top to bottom. This program has two statements; the first one asks the user for a number, and the second one shows the square of that number:

```
var theNumber = Number(prompt("Pick a number", ""));
alert("Your number is the square root of " + (theNumber * theNumber));
```

The function Number converts a value to a number, which is needed in this case because the result of prompt is a string value. There are similar functions called String and Boolean that convert values to those types.

Conditional Execution

Sometimes, you do not want all the statements in your program to always be executed in the same order. For example, in the previous program, we might want to show the square of the input only if the input is actually a number.

The keyword if can be used to execute or skip a statement depending on the value of a Boolean expression. We can do this:

```
var theNumber = Number(prompt("Pick a number", ""));
if (!isNaN(theNumber))
  alert("Your number is the square root of " + (theNumber * theNumber));
```

The condition expression (!isNaN(theNumber) in this case) is provided, in parentheses, after the word if. Only when this expression produces a true value, the statement after the if is executed.

When Number is called on something like "moo", which does not contain a number, the result will be the special value NaN, which stands for "not a number." The function isNaN is used to determine whether its argument is NaN, so !isNaN(theNumber) is true when theNumber is a proper number.

Often you have not only code that must be executed when a certain condition holds but also code that handles the other case, when the condition doesn't hold. The else keyword can be used, together with if, to create two separate, parallel paths that execution can take:

```
if (true == false)
  print("How confusing!");
else
  print("True still isn't false.");
```

If we have more than two paths that we want to choose from, multiple if/else pairs can be "chained" together. Here's an example:

```
var num = prompt("Pick a number:", "0");

if (num < 10)
  print("Small");
else if (num < 100)
  print("Medium");
else
  print("Large");
```

The program will first check whether num is less than 10. If it is, it chooses that branch, prints "Small", and is done. If it isn't, it takes the else branch, which itself contains a second if. If the second condition (< 100) holds, that means the number is between 10 and 100, and "Medium" is printed. If it doesn't, the second and last else branch is chosen.

while and do Loops

Consider a program that prints out all even numbers from 0 to 12. One way to write this is as follows:

```
print(0);
print(2);
print(4);
print(6);
print(8);
print(10);
print(12);
```

That works, but the idea of writing a program is to make something *less* work, not more. If we needed all even numbers less than 1,000, the previous would be unworkable. What we need is a way to automatically repeat some code.

```
var currentNumber = 0;
while (currentNumber <= 12) {
  print(currentNumber);
  currentNumber = currentNumber + 2;
}
```

A statement starting with the word while creates a *loop*. A loop, much like a conditional, is a disturbance in the sequence of statements—but rather than executing a statements either once or not at all, it may cause them to be repeated multiple times. The word while is followed by an expression in parentheses, which is used to determine whether the loop will loop or finish. As long as the Boolean value produced by this expression is true, the code in the loop is repeated. As soon as it is false, the program goes to the bottom of the loop and continues executing statements normally.

The variable currentNumber demonstrates the way a variable can track the progress of a program. Every time the loop repeats, it is incremented by 2. Then, at the beginning of every repetition, it is compared with the number 12 to decide whether the program has done all the work it has to do.

The third part of a while statement is another statement. This is the *body* of the loop, the action or actions that must take place multiple times. If we did not have to print the numbers, the program could have looked like this:

```
var currentNumber = 0;
while (currentNumber <= 12)
  currentNumber = currentNumber + 2;
```

Here, currentNumber = currentNumber + 2; is the statement that forms the body of the loop. We must also print the number, though, so the loop statement must consist of more than one statement. Braces ({ and }) are used to group statements into *blocks*. To the world outside the block, a block counts as a single statement. In the example, this is used to include in the loop both the call to print and the statement that updates currentNumber.

As an example that actually does something useful, we can write a program that calculates and shows the value of 2^{10} (2 to the 10th power). We use two variables: one to keep track of our result and one to count how often we have multiplied this result by 2. The loop tests whether the second variable has reached 10 yet and then updates both variables.

```
var result = 1;
var counter = 0;
while (counter < 10) {
  result = result * 2;
  counter = counter + 1;
}
result;
→ 1024
```

The counter could also start at 1 and check for <= 10, but, for reasons that will become apparent later, it is a good idea to get used to counting from 0.

A very similar control structure is the do loop. It differs only on one point from a while loop: it will execute its body at least once, and only then start testing whether it should stop. To reflect this, the test is written below the body of the loop:

```
do {
  var input = prompt("Who are you?");
} while (!input);
```

Indenting Code

You will have noticed the spaces I put in front of some statements. These are not required—the computer will accept the program just fine without them. In fact, even the line breaks in programs are optional. You could write them as a single long line if you felt like it. The role of the indentation inside blocks is to make the structure of the code stand out. Because new blocks can be opened inside other blocks, it can become hard to see where one block ends and another begins when looking at a complex piece of code. When lines are indented, the visual shape of a program corresponds to the shape of the blocks inside it. I like to use two spaces for every open block, but tastes differ—some people use four spaces, and some people use tabs.

for Loops

The uses of while we have seen so far all show the same pattern. First, a "counter" variable is created. This variable tracks the progress of the loop. The while itself contains a check, usually to see whether the counter has reached some boundary yet. Then, at the end of the loop body, the counter is updated.

A lot of loops fall into this pattern. For this reason, JavaScript, and similar languages, also provide a slightly shorter and more comprehensive form:

```
for (var number = 0; number <= 12; number = number + 2)
  print(number);
```

This program is exactly equivalent to the earlier even-number-printing example. The only change is that all the statements that are related to the "state" of the loop are now on one line. The parentheses after the for should contain two semicolons. The part before the first semicolon *initializes* the loop, usually by defining a variable. The second part is the expression that *checks* whether the loop must still continue. The final part *updates* the state of the loop. In most cases, this is shorter and clearer than a while construction.

Here is the code that computes 2^{10}, using for instead of while:

```
var result = 1;
for (var counter = 0; counter < 10; counter = counter + 1)
  result = result * 2;
result;
→ 1024
```

Note that even if no block is opened with a {, the statement in the loop is still indented two spaces to make it clear that it "belongs" to the line before it.

Breaking Out of a Loop

When a loop does not always have to go all the way through to its end, the break keyword can be useful. It is a statement that immediately jumps out of the current loop, continuing after it. This program finds the first number that is greater than 20 and divisible by 7:

```
for (var current = 20; ; current++) {
  if (current % 7 == 0)
    break;
}
current;
→ 21
```

The trick with the modulo (%) operator is an easy way to test whether a number is divisible by another number. If it is, the remainder of their division, which is what modulo gives you, is zero.

This for construct does not have a part that checks for the end of the loop. This means that it is dependent on the break statement inside it to ever stop. As an aside, the same loop could also have been written simply as follows:

```
for (var current = 20; current % 7 != 0; current++)
  ; // Do nothing.
```

In this case, the body of the loop is empty. A lone semicolon can be used to produce an empty statement.

Updating Variables Succinctly

A program, especially when looping, often needs to "update" a variable with a value that is based on its previous value, as in counter = counter + 1. JavaScript provides a shortcut for this: counter += 1. This also works for many other operators, as in result *= 2 to double the value of result or as in counter -= 1 to count downward.

For counter += 1 and counter -= 1, there are even shorter versions: counter++ and counter--.

Once again, the example becomes a little shorter:

```
var result = 1;
for (var counter = 0; counter < 10; counter++)
  result *= 2;
```

Dispatching on a Value with switch

It is common for code to look like this:

```
if (variable == "value1") action1();
else if (variable == "value2") action2();
else if (variable == "value3") action3();
else defaultAction();
```

There is a construct called switch that is intended to solve such a "dispatch" in a more direct way. Unfortunately, the syntax JavaScript uses for this (which it inherited from the C and Java line of programming languages) is somewhat awkward—sometimes a chain of if statements still looks better. Here is an example:

```
switch(prompt("What is the weather like?")) {
  case "rainy":
    print("Remember to bring an umbrella.");
    break;
  case "sunny":
    print("Dress lightly.");
  case "cloudy":
    print("Go outside.");
    break;
  default:
    print("Unknown weather type!");
    break;
}
```

Inside the block opened by switch, you may put any number of case labels. The program will jump to the label that corresponds to the value that switch was given, or to default if no matching value is found. Then it starts executing statements there, and *continues* past other labels, until it reaches a break statement. In some cases, such as the "sunny" case in the example, this can be used to share some code between cases (it recommends going outside for both sunny and cloudy weather). But beware, since it is very easy to forget such a break, which will cause the program to execute code you do not want executed.

Capitalization

I have been using some rather odd capitalization in my variable names. Because you cannot have spaces in these names—the computer would read them as two separate variables—your choices for writing a variable name that is made of several words are limited to the following: fuzzylittleturtle, fuzzy_little_turtle, FuzzyLittleTurtle, or fuzzyLittleTurtle. The first example is hard to read. Personally, I like using underscores, though it is a little painful to type. However, the standard JavaScript functions, and most

JavaScript programmers, follow the last example. It is not hard to get used to little things like that, so we will just follow the crowd and capitalize the first letter of every word after the first.

In a few cases, such as the Number function, the first letter of a variable is also capitalized. This was done to mark this function as a constructor. What a constructor is will become clear in Chapter 6. For now, the important thing is not to be bothered by this apparent lack of consistency.

Comments

In one of the example programs, I showed a part that said // Do nothing. This might have looked a bit suspicious to you. It is often useful to include extra text in a program. The most common use for this is adding some explanations to the program.

```
// The variable counter, which is about to be defined, is going
// to start with a value of 0, which is zero.
var counter = 0;
// Next, we loop. Hold on to your hat.
while (counter < 100 /* counter is less than one hundred */)
/* Every time we loop, we INCREMENT the value of counter,
   You could say we just add one to it. */
  counter++;
// And here, we are done.
```

This kind of text is called a *comment*. The rules are like this: /* starts a comment that goes on until a */ is found. // starts another kind of comment, which just goes until the end of the line.

As you can see, even the simplest programs can be made to look big, ugly, and complicated by adding a lot of comments to them. On the other hand, when a piece of code actually is difficult or confusing, a comment explaining its purpose and workings can help a lot.

More on Types

The previous should enable you to write and understand simple JavaScript programs. However, before closing the chapter, a few more subtleties have to be cleared up.

Undefined Values

It is possible to define a variable using var something;, without giving it a value. What happens when you take the value of such a variable?

```
var mysteryVariable;
mysteryVariable;
→ undefined
```

In terms of tentacles, this variable ends in thin air—it has nothing to grasp. When you ask for the value of an empty place, you get a special value named undefined. Functions that do not return a specific value but are called for their side effects, such as print and alert, also return an undefined value.

There is also a similar value, null, whose meaning is "this value is defined, but it does not have a value." The difference in meaning between undefined and null is mostly academic and usually not very interesting. In practical programs, it is often necessary to check whether something "has a value." In these cases, the expression something == undefined may be used, because even though they are not exactly the same value, the expression null == undefined will produce true.

Automatic Type Conversion

The previous brings us to another tricky subject. Consider the following expressions and the Boolean values they produce:

```
false == 0;
→ true
"" == 0;
→ true
"5" == 5;
→ true
```

When comparing values that have different types, JavaScript uses a complicated and confusing set of rules. I will not explain them precisely, but in most cases it just tries to convert one of the values to the type of the other value. However, when null or undefined occurs, it produces true only if both sides are null or undefined.

What if you want to test whether a variable refers to the value false? The rules for converting strings and numbers to Boolean values state that 0, NaN, and the empty string count as false, while all the other values count as true. Because of this, the expression variable == false is also true when variable refers to 0 or "". For cases like this, where you do *not* want any automatic type conversions to happen, there are two extra operators: === and !==. The first tests whether a value is precisely equal to the other, and the second tests whether it is not precisely equal. When rewritten to use ===, the expressions in the previous example will return false:

```
null === undefined;
→ false
false === 0;
→ false
"" === 0;
→ false
"5" === 5;
→ false
```

Values given as the condition in an `if`, `while`, or `for` statement do not have to be Booleans. They will be automatically converted to Booleans before they are checked. This means that the number `0`, the empty string `""`, `null`, `undefined`, `NaN`, and of course `false` will all count as false.

The fact that all other values are converted to true in this case makes it possible to leave out explicit comparisons in many situations. If a variable is known to contain either a string or `null`, one could check for this very simply:

```
var maybeNull = null;
// ... mystery code that might put a string into maybeNull ...
if (maybeNull)
  print("maybeNull has a value");
```

That would work except in the case where the mystery code gives `maybeNull` the value `""`. An empty string is false, so nothing is printed. Depending on what you are trying to do, this might be *wrong*. It is often a good idea to add an explicit `=== null` or `=== false` in cases like this to prevent subtle mistakes. The same occurs with number values that might be `0`.

Dangers of Automatic Type Conversion

There are some other situations that cause automatic type conversions to happen. If you add a nonstring value to a string, the value is automatically converted to a string before it is concatenated. If you multiply a number and a string, JavaScript tries to make a number out of the string.

```
"Apollo" + 5;
→ "Apollo5"
null + "ify";
→ "nullify"
"5" * 5;
→ 25
"strawberry" * 5;
→ NaN
```

The `NaN` in the previous example refers to the fact that a strawberry is not a number. All arithmetic operations on the value `NaN` result in `NaN`, which is why multiplying it by 5, as in the example, still gives a `NaN` value. Also, and this can be disorienting at times, `NaN == NaN` equals `false`. Checking whether a value is `NaN` can be done with `isNaN` function, as we saw before.

These automatic conversions can be very convenient, but they are also rather weird and error prone. Even though `+` and `*` are both arithmetic operators, they behave completely different in the example. In my own code, I use `+` on nonstrings a lot but make it a point not to use `*` and the other numeric operators on string values. Converting a number to a string is always possible and straightforward, but converting a string to a number may not even work (as in the last line of the example). We can use `Number` to explicitly convert the string to a number, making it clear that we might run the risk of getting a NaN value.

```
Number("5") * 5;
→ 25
```

More on && and ||

When we discussed the Boolean operators && and || earlier, I claimed they produced Boolean values. This turns out to be a bit of an oversimplification. If you apply them to Boolean values, they will indeed return Booleans. But they can also be applied to other kinds of values, in which case they will return one of their arguments.

What || really does is this: It looks at the value to the left of it first. If converting this value to a Boolean would produce true, it returns this left value, and otherwise it returns the one on its right. Check for yourself that this does the correct thing when the arguments are Booleans. Why does it work like that? It turns out this is very practical. Consider this example:

```
var input = prompt("What is your name?", "Kilgore Trout");
print("Well hello " + (input || "dear"));
```

If the user clicks Cancel or closes the prompt dialog box in some other way without giving a name, the variable input will hold the value null or "". Both of these would give false when converted to a Boolean. The expression input || "dear" can in this case be read as "the value of the variable input, or else the string "dear"." It is an easy way to provide a "fallback" value.

The && operator works similarly, but the other way around. When the value to its left is something that would give false when converted to a Boolean, it returns that value, and otherwise it returns the value on its right.

Another important property of these two operators is that the expression to their right is evaluated only when necessary. In the case of true || X, no matter what X is, the result will be true, so X is never evaluated, and if it has side effects, they never happen. The same goes for false && X. The following will show only a single alert window:

```
false || alert("I'm happening!");
false && alert("Not me.");
```

2

FUNCTIONS

We have already *used* several functions in the previous chapter—things such as alert and print—to order the machine to perform a specific operation. In this chapter, we will start *creating* our own functions, making it possible to extend the vocabulary that we have available. In a way, this resembles defining our own words inside a story we are writing to increase our expressiveness. Although such a thing is considered rather bad style in prose, in programming it is indispensable.

The Anatomy of a Function Definition

In its most basic form, a function definition looks like this:

```
function square(x) {
  return x * x;
}

square(12);
→ 144
```

Here, square is the name of the function. x is the name of its (first and only) argument. return x * x; is the body of the function.

The keyword function is always used when creating a new function. When it is followed by a variable name, the new function will be stored under this name. After the name comes a list of argument names and finally the body of the function. Unlike those around the body of while loops or if statements, the braces around a function body are obligatory.

The keyword return, followed by an expression, is used to determine the value the function returns. When control comes across a return statement, it immediately jumps out of the current function and gives the returned value to the code that called the function. A return statement without an expression after it will cause the function to return undefined.

A body can, of course, have more than one statement in it. Here is a function for computing powers (with positive, integer exponents):

```
function power(base, exponent) {
  var result = 1;
  for (var count = 0; count < exponent; count++)
    result *= base;
  return result;
}
```

```
power(2, 10);
→ 1024
```

The arguments to a function behave like variables—but ones that are given a value by the *caller* of the function, not the function itself. The function is free to give them a new value though, just like normal variables.

Definition Order

Even though function definitions occur as statements between the rest of the program, they are not part of the same timeline. In the following example, the first statement can call the future function, even though its definition comes later:

```
print("The future says: ", future());

function future() {
  return "We STILL have no flying cars.";
}
```

What is happening is that the computer looks up all function definitions, and stores the associated functions, *before* it starts executing the rest of the program. The nice thing about this is that we do not have to think about the order in which we define and use our functions—they are all allowed to call each other, regardless of which one is defined first.

Local Variables

A very important property of functions is that the variables created inside of them are *local* to the function. This means, for example, that the result variable in the power example will be newly created every time the function is called and will no longer exist after the function returns. In fact, if power were to call itself, that call would cause a *new*, distinct result variable to be created and used by the inner call and would leave the variable in the outer call untouched.

This "localness" of variables applies only to the arguments of the function and those variables that are declared with the var keyword inside the function. It is possible to access *global* (nonlocal) variables inside a function, as long as you haven't declared a local variable with the same name.

The following code demonstrates this. It defines (and calls) two functions that both change the value of the variable x. The first one does not declare the variable as local and thus changes the global variable defined at the start of the example. The second does declare it and ends up changing only the local variable.

```
var x = "A";

function setVarToB() {
  x = "B";
}
setVarToB();
x;
→ "B";

function setVarToC() {
  var x;
  x = "C";
}
setVarToC();
x;
→ "B";
```

As an aside, note that these functions contain no return statements, because they are called for their side effects, not to create a value. The actual return value of such functions is undefined.

Nested Scope

In JavaScript, it is not enough to simply distinguish between *global* and *local* variables. In fact, there can be any number of stacked (or nested) variable scopes. Functions defined inside other functions can refer to the local variables in their parent function, functions defined inside those inner functions can refer to variables in both their parent and their grandparent functions, and so on.

Take a look at this example. It defines a function that takes the absolute (positive) value of number and multiplies that by factor.

```
function multiplyAbsolute(number, factor) {
  function multiply(number) {
    return number * factor;
  }
  if (number < 0)
    return multiply(-number);
  else
    return multiply(number);
}
```

The example is intentionally confusing in order to demonstrate a subtlety—it contains two separate variables named number. When the body of the function multiply runs, it uses the same factor variable as the outer function but has its own number variable (created for the argument of that name). Thus, it multiplies its own argument by the factor passed to multiplyAbsolute.

What this comes down to is that the set of variables visible inside a function is determined by the place of that function in the program text. All variables that were defined "above" a function's definition are visible, which means both those in function bodies that enclose it and those at the top level of the program. This approach to variable visibility is called *lexical scoping*.

People who have experience with other programming languages might expect that a block of code (between braces) also produces a new local environment. Not in JavaScript. Functions are the only things that create a new scope. You are allowed to use free-standing blocks:

```
var something = 1;
{
  var something = 2;
  // Do stuff with variable something...
}
// Outside of the block again...
```

But the something inside the block refers to the same variable as the one outside the block. In fact, although blocks like this are allowed, they are only useful to group the body of an if statement or a loop. (Most people agree that this is a bit of a design blunder by the designers of JavaScript, and later versions of the language will add some way to define variables that stay inside blocks.)

The Stack

To understand how functions are called and how they return, it is useful to be aware of a thing called the *stack*. When a function is called, control is given to the body of that function. When that body returns, the code that called the function is resumed. Thus, while the body is running, the computer must remember the context from which the function was called so that it knows where to continue afterward. The place where this context is stored is the stack.

The reason that it is called a stack has to do with the fact that, as we saw, a function body can again call a function. Every time a function is called, another context has to be stored. One can visualize this as a stack of contexts. Every time a function is called, the current context is thrown on top of the stack. When a function returns, the context on top is taken off the stack and resumed.

This stack requires space in the computer's memory to be stored. When the stack grows too big, the computer will give up with a message like "out of stack space" or "too much recursion." The following code illustrates that—it asks the computer a really hard question, which causes an infinite back-and-forth between two functions. Or rather, it would be infinite, if we had an infinite stack. As it is, it will run out of space, or "blow the stack."

```
function chicken() {
  return egg();
}
function egg() {
  return chicken();
}
print(chicken() + " came first.");
```

Function Values

As I mentioned in the previous chapter, *everything* in JavaScript is a value, including functions. This means that the names of defined functions can be used like normal variables, and their content can be passed around and used in bigger expressions. The following example will call the function in variable a, unless that is a "false" value (like null), in which case it chooses and calls b instead.

```
var a = null;
function b() {return "B";}
(a || b)();
→ "B"
```

The bizarre-looking expression (a || b)() applies the "call without arguments" operation represented by () to the expression (a || b). If that expression does not produce a function value, this will of course produce an error. But when it does, as in the example, the resulting value is called, and all is well.

When we simply need an unnamed function value, the function keyword can be used as an expression, like this:

```
var a = null;
(a || function(){return "B";})();
→ "B"
```

This produces the same effect as the previous example, except that this time no function named b is defined. The "nameless" (or "anonymous") function expression function(){return "B";} simply creates a function value. It is possible to specify arguments or multistatement bodies in such definitions as well.

In Chapter 5, the *first-class* nature of functions (which is the usual term used for the "functions are values" concept) will be further explored and used to write some very clever code.

Closure

The nature of the function stack, combined with the ability to treat functions as values, brings up an interesting question. What happens to local variables when the function call that created them is no longer on the stack? The following code illustrates this:

```
function createFunction() {
  var local = 100;
  return function(){return local;};
}
```

When createFunction is called, it creates a local variable and then returns a function that returns this local variable. The question of how to treat this situation is known as the "upwards Funarg problem," and many old programming languages simply forbid it. JavaScript, fortunately, is from a generation of languages that solve this problem by going out of their way to preserve the local variable as long as it is in any way reachable. Doing createFunction()() (creating the function and then calling it) results in the value 100 being returned, as hoped.

This feature is called *closure,* and a function that "closes over" some local variables is called *a closure.* This behavior not only frees you from having to worry about variables still being "alive" but also allows for some creative use of function values.

For example, the following function makes it possible to dynamically create function values that add a certain number to their argument:

```
function makeAdder(amount) {
  return function(number) {
    return number + amount;
  };
}

var addTwo = makeAdder(2);
addTwo(3);
→ 5
```

Optional Arguments

It turns out we can execute the following code:

```
alert("Hello", "Good Evening", "How do you do?", "Good-bye");
```

The function alert officially accepts only one argument. Yet when you call it like this, it does not complain. It simply ignores the other arguments and shows you Hello.

JavaScript is notoriously nonstrict about the amount of arguments you pass to a function. If you pass too many, the extra ones are ignored. If you pass too few, the missing ones get the value undefined. The downside of this is that it is possible—even likely—that you'll accidentally pass the wrong number of arguments to functions, and no one will tell you about it.

The upside of this is that it can be used to have a function take "optional arguments." For example, this version of power can be called with only a single argument, in which case it behaves like square:

```
function power(base, exponent) {
  var result = 1;
  if (exponent === undefined)
    exponent = 2;
  for (var count = 0; count < exponent; count++)
    result *= base;
  return result;
}
```

In the next chapter, we will see a way in which a function body can get at the exact list of arguments that were passed to it. This can be useful, because it makes it possible to have a function accept any number of arguments. print makes use of this—the following prints R2D2:

```
print("R", 2, "D", 2);
```

Techniques

Now that we have a rather good idea of what JavaScript functions are and how they function, we will look at some considerations that come into play when designing and writing them.

Avoiding Repetition

The reason functions were invented is to reuse pieces of code. Programs typically need to perform the same operation (such as exponentiation) multiple times, and when you repeat the full code needed to perform the operation every time you need it, your program is going to be a lot longer.

Not only will it be longer, but it will also be more boring to read and more likely to contain errors. For example, the power function we defined does not work with negative exponents. If you find out that those are also needed, you'd have to update all the places where you take the power of a number and fix them. If you defined a function, all it takes is fixing the function, and all uses of it will suddenly work correctly.

When finding you need the same piece of code more than once and deciding to move it into a function, you need to determine how much of the code should go into the function and what the interface to the function should look like. For example, say we have some code to print a zero-padded number, like this:

```
var number = 5;
if (number < 10)
  print("0", number);
else
  print(number);
```

But it turns out we need to print padded numbers in other places as well. We now have several choices to make.

Do we make a function at all? The occurrences of the code might be in different projects, making it more work to share functions. Usually, the answer to this is "yes," regardless.

Does the function include the printing action, or does it just produce a zero-padded string? The best functions are those that perform a single, simple action, since they are easier to name (and thus easier to understand) and can be used in a wider variety of situations. So, write a zeroPad function, rather than a printZeroPadded function. print(zeroPad(5)) is no harder to type than printZeroPadded(5), after all.

How smart and versatile should the function be? We could write anything from a terribly simple "pad this number with a single zero" function to an involved formatted-output system that handles fractional numbers, rounding, and table layout. A good principle is to not add cleverness unless you are absolutely sure you are going to need it. It is tempting to fall into the trap of writing complicated "frameworks" for every little bit of functionality you need and never getting any actual work done. In this case, a second argument that specifies the width of the resulting number sounds like a useful, simple addition.

```
function zeroPad(number, width) {
  var string = String(Math.round(number));
  while (string.length < width)
    string = "0" + string;
  return string;
}
```

Math.round is a function that rounds a number; String is a function that converts its argument to a string.

Purity

"Purity," when applied to functions, is not about their lack of contaminants or their sexual behavior, but about whether they have side effects. *Pure functions* are the things that mathematicians mean when they say "function." They always return the same value when given the same arguments and do not have side effects.

The distinction between pure and nonpure functions is interesting mostly in terms of good code design and mental overhead. If a function is pure, a call to it can be mentally substituted by its result without changing the meaning of the code. When you are not sure that it is working correctly, you can test it by simply calling it and know that if it works in that context, it will work in any context. Nonpure functions might return different values based on all kinds of factors and have side effects that might be hard to test and think about.

Because pure functions are self-sufficient, they are likely to be useful and relevant in a wider range of situations than nonpure ones. Take the zeroPad function that we wrote earlier, for example. Had we written printZeroPadded instead, the function would have been useful only in situations where a print function had been defined and where we wanted to directly print our padded number. When defined as a pure function from a number to a string, the function depends on less context and is more generally applicable.

Of course, zeroPad solves a different problem than print, and no pure function is going to be able to do what print does, because it requires a side effect. In many cases, nonpure functions are precisely what you need. In other cases, a problem can be solved with a pure function, but the nonpure variant is much more convenient or efficient. Generally, when something can naturally be expressed as a pure function, write it that way. You'll thank yourself later. If not, don't feel dirty for writing nonpure functions.

Recursion

As mentioned earlier, it is valid for a function to call itself. A function that calls itself is called *recursive*. Recursion allows for some interesting function definitions. Look at this alternate implementation of power:

```
function power(base, exponent) {
  if (exponent == 0)
    return 1;
  else
    return base * power(base, exponent - 1);
}
```

This is rather close to the way mathematicians define exponentiation, and conceptually it looks a lot nicer than the earlier version. It sort of loops, but there is no while, for, or even a local side effect to be seen. By calling itself, the function produces the same effect that was produced with a for loop before.

There is one important problem: In most JavaScript implementations, this second version is about 10 times slower than the first one. In JavaScript, running through a simple loop is a *lot* cheaper than calling a function multiple times. On top of that, using a sufficiently large exponent to this function might cause the stack to overflow.

The dilemma of speed versus elegance is an interesting one and is not limited to debates about recursion. In many situations, an elegant, intuitive, and often short solution can be replaced by a more convoluted but faster solution.

In the case of the earlier power function, the inelegant version is still sufficiently simple and easy to read. It does not make much sense to replace it with the recursive version. Often, though, the concepts a program is dealing with get so complex that giving up some efficiency in order to make the program more straightforward becomes an attractive choice.

The basic rule, which has been repeated by many programmers and with which I wholeheartedly agree, is to not worry about efficiency until your program is provably too slow. When it is, find out which parts are taking up the most time, and start exchanging elegance for efficiency in those parts.

Of course, the previous rule doesn't mean one should start ignoring performance altogether. In many cases, like the power function, not much simplicity is gained by the "elegant" approach. In other cases, an experienced programmer can see right away that a simple approach is never going to be fast enough.

The reason I am making a big deal out of this is that surprisingly many programmers focus fanatically on efficiency, even in the smallest details. The result is bigger, more complicated, and often less correct programs, which take longer to write than their more straightforward equivalents and often run only marginally faster.

Recursion is not always just a less-efficient alternative to looping. Some problems are much easier to solve with recursion than with loops. Most often these are problems that require exploring or processing several "branches," each of which might branch out again into more branches.

Consider this puzzle: By starting from the number 1 and repeatedly either adding 5 or multiplying by 3, an infinite amount of new numbers can be produced. How would you write a function that, given a number, tries to find a sequence of additions and multiplications that produce that number?

For example, the number 13 could be reached by first multiplying 1 by 3 and then adding 5 twice. The number 15 cannot be reached at all.

Here is the solution:

```
function findSequence(goal) {
  function find(start, history) {
    if (start == goal)
      return history;
    else if (start > goal)
      return null;
    else
      return find(start + 5, "(" + history + " + 5)") ||
             find(start * 3, "(" + history + " * 3)");
  }
  return find(1, "1");
}
```

```
findSequence(24);
→ (((1 * 3) + 5) * 3)
```

Note that it doesn't necessarily find the *shortest* sequence of operations—it is satisfied when it finds any sequence at all.

How does it work? The inner find function, by calling itself in two different ways, explores both the possibility of adding 5 to the current number and of multiplying it by 3. When it finds the number, it returns the history string, which is used to record all the operations that were performed to get to this number. It also checks whether the current number is bigger than goal. If it is, we should stop exploring this branch, since it is not going to give us our number.

The use of the || operator in the example can be read as "return the solution found by adding 5 to start, and if that fails, return the solution found by multiplying start by 3." Equivalent (but more wordy) code would look like this:

```
else {
  var found = find(start + 5, "(" + history + " + 5)");
  if (found == null)
    found = find(start * 3, "(" + history + " * 3)");
  return found;
}
```

3

DATA STRUCTURES: OBJECTS AND ARRAYS

In this chapter, we will solve a programming problem that involves extracting data from text. In the process, we learn about object values and arrays and how to use them.

The Problem: Aunt Emily's Cats

Consider the following situation: Your crazy Aunt Emily, who is rumored to have more than 50 cats living with her (you never managed to count them), regularly sends you emails to keep you up-to-date on her exploits. They usually look like this:

> Dear nephew,
>
> Your mother told me you have taken up skydiving. Is this true? You watch yourself, young man! Remember what happened to my husband? And that was only from the second floor!
>
> Anyway, things are very exciting here. I have spent all week trying to get the attention of Mr. Drake, the nice gentleman who moved in next door, but I think he is afraid of cats. Or allergic to them?

I am going to try putting Fat Igor on his shoulder next time I see him, very curious what will happen.

Also, the scam I told you about is going better than expected. I have already gotten back five "payments," and only one complaint. It is starting to make me feel a bit bad though. And you are right that it is probably illegal in some way.

[etc., etc.]

Much love,
Aunt Emily

died 27/04/2006: Black Leclère

born 05/04/2006 (mother Lady Penelope): Red Lion, Doctor Hobbles the 3rd, Little Iroquois

To humor the old dear, you would like to keep track of the genealogy of her cats, so you can add things like "P.S. I hope Doctor Hobbles the 2nd enjoyed his birthday this Saturday!" or "How is old Lady Penelope doing? She's five years old now, isn't she?"—preferably without accidentally asking about dead cats. You are in the possession of a large quantity of old emails from your aunt, and fortunately she is very consistent in always putting information about the cats' births and deaths at the end of her emails in precisely the same format.

You are, of course, lazy and hardly inclined to go through all those emails by hand. But we are, coincidentally, just in need of an example problem. Let's try to work out a program that does the work for us. For a start, we will write a program that gives us a list of cats that are still alive after the most recent email.

(Before you ask, at the start of the correspondence, Aunt Emily had only a single cat: Spot. She was still rather conventional in those days.)

It usually pays to have some kind of clue what one's program is going to do before starting to type. Here's a plan:

1. Start with a set of cat names that has only "Spot" in it.

2. Go over every email in our archive, in chronological order.

3. Look for paragraphs that start with "born" or "died."

4. Add the names from paragraphs that start with "born" to our set of names.

5. Remove the names from paragraphs that start with "died" from our set.

Taking the names from a paragraph goes like this:

1. Find the colon in the paragraph.

2. Take the part after this colon.

3. Split this part into separate names by looking for commas.

It may require some suspension of disbelief to accept that Aunt Emily always uses this exact format, and that she never forgets or misspells a name, but that is just how your aunt is.

Basic Data Structures

Before we can write this program, we will need to go over a few new language features.

Properties

Some JavaScript values have other values associated with them. These associations are called *properties*. Every string, for example, has a property called length, which refers to an integer, the amount of characters in that string.

Properties can be accessed in two ways, either with brackets or using dot notation:

```
var text = "purple haze";
text["length"];
→ 11
text.length;
→ 11
```

The second way is a shorthand for the first, and it works only when the name of the property is a valid variable name—when it doesn't have any spaces or symbols in it and does not start with a digit character.

Trying to read a property from the values null and undefined will cause an error. Numbers and Booleans do have properties, but none of them is interesting or useful enough to be discussed here.

Object Values

In most value types, if they have properties at all, they are fixed, and you are not allowed to change them. (A string's length always stays the same, for example.) However, there is one type of value, *objects*, where properties can be freely added, removed, and changed. The main role of objects, in fact, is to be a collection of properties.

An object can be written like this:

```
var cat = {color: "gray", name: "Spot", size: 46};
cat.size = 47;
cat.size;
→ 47
delete cat.size;
cat.size;
→ undefined
```

Like variables, each property attached to an object is labeled by a name. Property names can be any strings, though, not just those that are valid variable names. The first statement creates an object in which the property "color" refers to the string "gray", the property "name" to the string "Spot", and the property "size" to the number 46. The second statement gives the property named size a new value, which is done in the same way as modifying a variable.

Trying to read a nonexistent property gives the value undefined. The keyword delete is used to cut off properties.

If a property that does not yet exist is set with the = operator, it is added to the object, as in the following example:

```
var empty = {};
empty.notReally = 1000;
empty;
→ {notReally: 1000}
```

Properties whose names are not valid variable names cannot be accessed with the dot notation, but only using brackets. When creating an object, these have to be quoted, unless they are numbers:

```
var thing = {"gabba gabba": "hey", 5: 10};
thing["5"];
→ 10
thing[2 + 3];
→ 10
delete thing["gabba gabba"];
```

The part between the brackets can be any expression. It is converted to a string to determine the property name it refers to. Thus, you can also use variables to name properties:

```
var propertyName = "length";
var text = "coco";
text[propertyName];
→ 4
```

The operator in can be used to test whether an object has a certain property. It produces a Boolean.

```
var chineseBox = {};
chineseBox.content = chineseBox;
"content" in chineseBox;
→ true
"content" in chineseBox.content;
→ true
```

Objects as Sets

The solution for the cat problem talks about a *set* of names. A set is a collection of values in which no value occurs more than once. If names are strings, can you think of a way to use an object to represent a set of names?

The idea, of course, would be to use the names as property names. To add a name to the set, we set the property in the object to some value (any value). Removing a name from the set is done by deleting the property. The in operator can be used to determine whether a certain name is part of the set. (There are a few subtle problems with using in like this, which we will discuss in Chapter 6. For now, it works well enough.)

Here we create a set containing only "Spot", add "White Fang" to it, delete "Spot" again, and finally, test whether "Asoka" is in it:

```
var set = {"Spot": true};
set["White Fang"] = true;
delete set["Spot"];
"Asoka" in set;
→ false
```

Mutability

Object values can apparently change. The types of values discussed in Chapter 1 are all *immutable*—it is impossible to change an existing value of those types. You can combine them and derive new values from them, but when you take a specific string value, the text inside it cannot change. With objects, on the other hand, the content of a value *can* be modified, by changing its properties.

When we have two numbers, 120 and 120, they can, whether they refer to the same physical bits or not, be considered the precise same number. With objects, there is a difference between having two references to the same object and having two different objects that contain the same properties. Consider the following code:

```
var object1 = {value: 10};
var object2 = object1;
var object3 = {value: 10};

object1 == object2;
→ true
object1 == object3;
→ false

object1.value = 15;
object2.value;
→ 15
object3.value;
→ 10
```

object1 and object2 are two variables grasping the *same* value. There is only one actual object, which is why changing object1 also changes the value of object2. The variable object3 points to another object, which initially contains the same properties as object1 but lives a separate life.

JavaScript's == operator, when comparing objects, will return true only if both values given to it are the precise same value. Comparing different object with identical contents will give false. This is useful in some situations but unpractical in others, where you have to write separate functions to compare objects by content.

Objects as Collections: Arrays

Object values can play a lot of different roles. Behaving like a set is only one of those. We will see a few other roles in this chapter, and Chapter 6 shows another important way of using objects.

The plan for the cat problem—in fact, let's call it an *algorithm*, not a plan—talks about going over all the emails in an archive. What kind of value could represent such an archive?

It should contain a number of emails. An email can simply be a string, for our purposes. We need to collect multiple strings into a single value. Well, collections are what objects are used for. As a first draft, one could make an object like this:

```
var mailArchive = {"the first email": "Dear nephew, ...",
                   "the second email": "..."
                   /* and so on ... */};
```

But that makes it hard to go over the emails from start to end—how does the program guess the name of these properties? This can be solved by more predictable property names:

```
var mailArchive = {0: "Dear nephew, ... (mail number 1)",
                   1: "(mail number 2)",
                   2: "(mail number 3)"};

for (var current = 0; current in mailArchive; current++)
  print("Processing email #", current, ": ", mailArchive[current]);
```

Luck has it that there is a special kind of objects specifically for this kind of use. They are called *arrays*, and they provide some conveniences, such as a length property that tells us how many values the array holds.

New arrays can be created using brackets ([and]):

```
var mailArchive = ["mail one", "mail two", "mail three"];

for (var current = 0; current < mailArchive.length; current++)
  print("Processing email #", current, ": ", mailArchive[current]);
```

In this example, the numbers of the elements are not specified explicitly any more. The first one automatically gets the number 0, the second the number 1, and so on.

Why start at 0? People tend to start counting from 1. As unintuitive as it seems, numbering the elements in a collection from 0 is how things have traditionally been done in most programming languages. Just go with it for now—it will grow on you.

Starting at element 0 also means that in a collection with X elements, the last element can be found at position X - 1. This is why the for loop in the example checks for current < mailArchive.length. There is no element at position mailArchive.length, so as soon as current has that value, we stop looping.

As an exercise, let's write a function range, which takes one argument—a positive number—and returns an array containing all numbers from 0 up to and including the given number.

An empty array can be created by simply typing []. Just like with objects, we can add elements to arrays by simply assigning to its properties. Since the element properties are numbers, we have to use [and], rather than the dot, to refer to them. (Note that the length property of the array will automatically get updated when elements are added or removed—it always holds the highest index that contains an element, plus one.)

```
function range(upto) {
  var result = [];
  for (var i = 0; i <= upto; i++)
    result[i] = i;
  return result;
}
range(4);
→ [0, 1, 2, 3, 4]
```

Instead of naming the loop variable counter or current, as I have been doing so far, it is here called simply i. Using single letters—usually i, j, and k—for loop variables is a widely spread habit among programmers. It has its origin mostly in laziness: We'd rather type one character than seven, and names like counter and current do not really clarify the meaning of the variable much.

If a program uses too many meaningless single-letter variables, it can become very confusing. In my own programs, I try to only do this in a few common cases. Small loops are one of these cases. If the loop contains another loop and if that one also uses a variable named i, the inner loop will modify the variable that the outer loop is using, and everything will break. One could use j for the inner loop, but in general, when the body of a loop is big, you should come up with meaningful name for your counter variable.

Methods

Both string and array objects contain, in addition to the `length` property, a number of properties that refer to function values.

```
var doh = "Doh";
typeof doh.toUpperCase;
→ "function"
doh.toUpperCase();
→ "DOH"
```

Every string has a `toUpperCase` property. When called, it will return a copy of the string, in which all letters have been converted to uppercase. There is also `toLowerCase`. You can guess what that does.

Notice that, even though the call to `toUpperCase` does not pass any arguments, the function does somehow have access to the string `"Doh"`, the value of which it is a property. How this works precisely is described in Chapter 6.

Properties that contain functions are generally called *methods*, as in "`toUpperCase` is a method of a string object." This example demonstrates some methods of array objects:

```
var mack = [];
mack.push("Mack");
mack.push("the");
mack.push("Knife");
mack;
→ ["Mack", "the", "Knife"]
mack.join(" ");
→ "Mack the Knife"
mack.pop();
→ "Knife"
mack;
→ ["Mack", "the"]
```

The method `push`, which is associated with arrays, can be used to insert values at the end of the array. It could have been used in the `range` function, replacing `result[i] = i` with `result.push(i)`. Then there is `pop`, the inverse of `push`: It takes out and returns the last value in the array. `join` builds a single big string from an array of strings. The parameter it is given is pasted between the values in the array.

Solving the Problem of Aunt Emily's Cats

Coming back to those cats, we now know that an array would be a good way to store the archive of emails. If we assume that we have an array of email strings in the variable `ARCHIVE`, going over all the emails is simple now:

```
for (var i = 0; i < ARCHIVE.length; i++) {
  var email = ARCHIVE[i];
  // Do something with this email...
}
```

We have also decided on a way to represent the set of cats that are alive. The next problem, then, is to find the paragraphs in an email that start with "born" or "died."

Separating Paragraphs

The first question that comes up is what exactly a paragraph is. In this case, the string value itself can't help us much: JavaScript's concept of text does not go any deeper than the "sequence of characters" idea, so we must define paragraphs in those terms.

In Chapter 1, we saw that there is such a thing as a newline character. These are what people typically use to split paragraphs. We consider a paragraph, then, to be part of an email that starts at a newline character or at the start of the content and that ends at the next newline character or at the end of the content.

And we don't even have to write the algorithm for splitting a string into paragraphs ourselves. Strings conveniently have a method named split, which is (almost) the opposite of the join method of arrays. It splits a string into an array, using the string given as its argument to determine in which places to cut. For example:

```
var words = "Cities of the Interior";
words.split(" ");
→ ["Cities", "of", "the", "Interior"]
```

Thus, cutting on newlines (email.split("\n")), can be used to split an email into paragraphs.

Finding Relevant Paragraphs

Paragraphs that do not start with either "born" or "died" can be ignored by the program. How do we test whether a string starts with a certain word? The method charAt can be used to get a specific character from a string. x.charAt(0) gives the first character, 1 is the second one, and so on. Thus, one way to check whether a string starts with "born" is as follows:

```
var paragraph = "born 15-11-2003 (mother Spot): White Fang";
paragraph.charAt(0) == "b" && paragraph.charAt(1) == "o" &&
  paragraph.charAt(2) == "r" && paragraph.charAt(3) == "n";
→ true
```

But that gets a bit clumsy—imagine checking for a word of 10 characters. There is something to be learned here, though: When a line gets ridiculously long, it can be spread over multiple lines. The result can be made easier to read by indenting the second line to show that it belongs together with the one above it.

Strings also have a method called slice. This copies out a piece of the string, starting from the character at the position given by the first argument and ending before (not including) the character at the position given by the second one. This method allows the check to be written in a shorter way:

```
paragraph.slice(0, 4) == "born";
→ true
```

We then wrap this approach in a function called startsWith, which takes two arguments, both strings. It returns true when the first argument starts with the characters in the second argument, and false otherwise.

```
function startsWith(string, pattern) {
  return string.slice(0, pattern.length) == pattern;
}

startsWith("rotation", "rot");
→ true
```

What happens when charAt or slice are used to take a piece of a string that does not exist? Will the startsWith function still work when the pattern is longer than the string it is matched against?

```
"Pip".charAt(250);
→ ""
"Nop".slice(1, 10);
→ "op"
```

charAt will return "" when there is no character at the given position, and slice will simply leave out the part of the new string that does not exist.

So yes, that means our version of startsWith works when, for example, startsWith("Idiots", "Most honored colleagues") is called. If pattern is longer than string, the call to slice will always return a string that is shorter than pattern (because string does not have enough characters). Because of that, the comparison with == will return false, which is correct.

It helps to always take a moment to consider abnormal (but valid) inputs for a program. These are usually called *corner cases*, and it is very common for programs that work perfectly on all the "regular" inputs to screw up on corner cases.

Extracting Cat Names

The only part of the cat problem that is still unsolved is the extraction of names from a paragraph. The algorithm, as shown before, was this:

1. Find the colon in the paragraph.

2. Take the part after this colon.

3. Split this part into separate names by looking for commas.

This has to happen both for paragraphs that start with "died" and paragraphs that start with "born." It would be a good idea to put it into a function so that the two pieces of code that handle these different kinds of paragraphs can both use it.

Strings have an indexOf method that can be used to find the (first) position of a character or substring within that string. Also, when slice is given only one argument, it will return the part of the string from the given position all the way to the end.

Thus, we can extract the names of the cats like this:

```
function catNames(paragraph) {
  var colon = paragraph.indexOf(":");
  return paragraph.slice(colon + 2).split(", ");
}
```

```
catNames("born 20/09/2004 (mother Yellow Bess): Doctor Hobbles the 2nd, Noog");
→ ["Doctor Hobbles the 2nd", "Noog"]
```

The informal description of the algorithm ignored the fact that there are spaces after the colon and the commas. The + 2 used when slicing the string is needed to leave out the colon itself and the space after it. The argument to split contains both a comma and a space, because that is what the names are really separated by, rather than just a comma.

This function does not do any checking for problems. We assume, here, that the input is always correct.

The Full Algorithm

All that remains now is putting the pieces together. One way to do that looks like this:

```
var livingCats = {"Spot": true};

for (var mail = 0; mail < ARCHIVE.length; mail++) {
  var paragraphs = ARCHIVE[mail].split("\n");
  for (var i = 0; i < paragraphs.length; i++) {
    var paragraph = paragraphs[i];
    if (startsWith(paragraph, "born")) {
      var names = catNames(paragraph);
      for (var name = 0; name < names.length; name++)
```

```
          livingCats[names[name]] = true;
      }
    else if (startsWith(paragraph, "died")) {
      var names = catNames(paragraph);
      for (var name = 0; name < names.length; name++)
        delete livingCats[names[name]];
    }
  }
}
```

That is quite a dense chunk of code. We'll look into making it prettier in a moment. But first let's look at our results. We know how to check whether a specific cat survives:

```
if ("Spot" in livingCats)
  print("Spot lives!");
else
  print("Good old Spot, may she rest in peace.");
```

But how do we list all the cats that are alive? The in keyword has a somewhat different meaning when it is used together with for:

```
for (var cat in livingCats)
  print(cat);
```

A loop like that will go over the names of the properties in an object, which allows us to enumerate all the names in our set.

Cleaning Up the Code

Some pieces of code can look like an impenetrable jungle. The example solution to the cat problem suffers from this. One way to make some light shine through it is to just add some strategic blank lines. This makes it look better but doesn't really solve the problem.

What is needed here is to break up the code. We already wrote two helper functions, startsWith and catNames, which both take care of a small, understandable part of the problem. Let's continue doing this.

```
function addToSet(set, values) {
  for (var i = 0; i < values.length; i++)
    set[values[i]] = true;
}

function removeFromSet(set, values) {
  for (var i = 0; i < values.length; i++)
    delete set[values[i]];
}
```

These two functions take care of the adding and removing of names from the set. That already cuts out the two most inner loops from the solution:

```
var livingCats = {Spot: true};

for (var mail = 0; mail < ARCHIVE.length; mail++) {
  var paragraphs = ARCHIVE[mail].split("\n");
  for (var i = 0; i < paragraphs.length; i++) {
    var paragraph = paragraphs[i];
    if (startsWith(paragraph, "born"))
      addToSet(livingCats, catNames(paragraph));
    else if (startsWith(paragraph, "died"))
      removeFromSet(livingCats, catNames(paragraph));
  }
}
```

Quite an improvement, if I may say so myself.

Why do addToSet and removeFromSet take the set as an argument? They could use the variable livingCats directly, if they wanted to. This way, they are not completely tied to our current problem. If addToSet directly changed livingCats, it would have to be called addCatsToCatSet, or something similar. The way it is now, it is a more generally useful tool.

Even if we are never going to use these functions for anything else, which is quite probable, it is useful to write them like this. Because they are "self-sufficient," they can be read and understood on their own, without needing to know about some external variable called livingCats.

The functions are not pure: They change the object passed as their set argument. This makes them slightly trickier than real pure functions, but they are still a lot less confusing than functions that run amok and change any value or variable they please.

We continue breaking the algorithm into pieces:

```
function findLivingCats() {
  var livingCats = {"Spot": true};

  function handleParagraph(paragraph) {
    if (startsWith(paragraph, "born"))
      addToSet(livingCats, catNames(paragraph));
    else if (startsWith(paragraph, "died"))
      removeFromSet(livingCats, catNames(paragraph));
  }

  for (var mail = 0; mail < ARCHIVE.length; mail++) {
    var paragraphs = ARCHIVE[mail].split("\n");
    for (var i = 0; i < paragraphs.length; i++)
      handleParagraph(paragraphs[i]);
  }
```

```
    return livingCats;
}
```

The whole algorithm is now encapsulated by a function. This means that it does not leave a mess after it runs: livingCats is a local variable in the function, instead of a top-level one, so it exists only while the function runs. The code that needs this set can call findLivingCats and use the value it returns.

It seemed to me that making handleParagraph a separate function also cleared things up. But this one is so closely tied to the cat algorithm that it is meaningless in any other situation. On top of that, it needs access to the livingCats variable. Thus, it is a perfect candidate to be a function-inside-a-function. When it lives inside findLivingCats, it is clear that it is relevant there only, and it has access to the variables of its parent function.

This solution is actually *bigger* than the previous one. Still, it is tidier, and I hope you'll agree that it is easier to read.

```
var howMany = 0;
for (var cat in findLivingCats())
  howMany++;
print("There are currently ", howMany, " cats alive.");
```

Date Representation

The program still ignores a lot of the information that is contained in the emails. There are birth dates, dates of death, and the names of mothers in there.

We'll start with the dates. What would be a good way to store a date? We could make an object with three properties, year, month, and day, and store numbers in them.

```
var when = {year: 1980, month: 2, day: 1};
```

But JavaScript already provides a kind of object for this purpose. Such an object can be created by using the keyword new:

```
var when = new Date(1980, 1, 1);
```

Just like the notation with braces and semicolons we have already seen, new is a way to create object values. Instead of specifying all the property names and values, a function is used to build up the object. This makes it possible to define a kind of standard procedure for creating objects. Functions like this are called *constructors*, and in Chapter 6 we will see how to write them ourselves.

The Date constructor can be used in different ways:

```
// Produces a date object for the current time.
new Date();
```

```
// February (!) 1st, 1980
new Date(1980, 1, 1);
// March 30th, 2007, 30 seconds past 8:20
new Date(2007, 2, 30, 8, 20, 30);
```

As you can see, these objects can store a time of day as well as a date. When not given any arguments, an object representing the current time and date is created. Arguments can be given to ask for a specific date and time. The order of the arguments is year, month, day, hour, minute, second, milliseconds. These last four are optional—they default to 0 when not specified.

The month numbers these objects use go from 0 to 11, which can be confusing, especially since day numbers *do* start from 1.

Date objects can be inspected with a number of get methods:

```
var today = new Date();
print("Year: ", today.getFullYear(), ", month: ",
      today.getMonth(), ", day: ", today.getDate());
print("Hour: ", today.getHours(), ", minutes: ",
      today.getMinutes(), ", seconds: ", today.getSeconds());
print("Day of week: ", today.getDay());
```

All of these, except for getDay, also have a set... variant that can be used to change the value of the date object.

Inside the object, a date is represented by the amount of milliseconds it is away from January 1, 1970. You can imagine this is quite a large number.

```
var today = new Date();
today.getTime();
→ 1266587282246
```

A very useful thing to do with dates is to compare them:

```
var wende = new Date(1989, 10, 9);
var gulfWarOne = new Date(1990, 6, 2);
wende < gulfWarOne;
→ true
wende == wende;
→ true
// but be careful...
wende == new Date(1989, 10, 9);
→ false
```

Comparing dates with <, >, <=, and >= does exactly what you would expect. When a date object is compared to itself with ==, the result is true, which is also good. But when == is used to compare a date object to a different, equal date object, we get false. Argh!

As mentioned earlier, == will return false when comparing two different objects, even if they contain the same properties. This is a bit clumsy and error prone here, since one would expect >= and == to behave in a more or less similar way. Testing whether two dates are equal can be done like this:

```
var wende1 = new Date(1989, 10, 9),
    wende2 = new Date(1989, 10, 9);
wende1.getTime() == wende2.getTime();
→ true
```

In addition to a date and time, Date objects also contain information about a time zone. When it is 1 p.m. in Amsterdam, it can, depending on the time of year, be 12 p.m. (noon) in London, and 7 a.m. in New York. Such times can only be compared when you take their time zones into account. The getTimezoneOffset function of a Date can be used to find out how many minutes it differs from Greenwich mean time (GMT). In Berlin, we get the following:

```
new Date().getTimezoneOffset();
→ -60
```

Date Extraction

The date part is always in the exact same place of a paragraph. How convenient.

```
"born 02/04/2001 (mother Clementine): Bugeye, Wolverine"
"died 27/04/2006: Black Leclère"
```

We can write a function extractDate that, given such a paragraph, returns a date object:

```
function extractDate(paragraph) {
  function numberAt(start, length) {
    return Number(paragraph.slice(start, start + length));
  }
  return new Date(numberAt(11, 4), numberAt(8, 2) - 1, numberAt(5, 2));
}
```

It would work without the calls to Number, but as mentioned in Chapter 1, I prefer not to use strings as if they are numbers. The inner function was introduced to prevent having to repeat the Number and slice part three times.

Note the - 1 for the month number. Like most people, Aunt Emily counts her months from 1, so we have to adjust the value before giving it to the Date constructor. (The day number does not have this problem, since Date objects count days in the usual human way.)

In Chapter 8 we will see a more practical and robust way of extracting information from strings.

Gathering More Information

Storing cats will work differently from now on. Instead of just putting the value true into the set, we store an object with information about the cat. When a cat dies, we do not remove it from the set; we just add a property death to the object to store the date on which the creature died.

This means our addToSet and removeFromSet functions have become useless. Something similar is needed, but it must also store birth dates and, later, the mother's name.

```
function catRecord(name, birthdate, mother) {
  return {name: name, birth: birthdate, mother: mother};
}

function addCats(set, names, birthdate, mother) {
  for (var i = 0; i < names.length; i++)
    set[names[i]] = catRecord(names[i], birthdate, mother);
}
function deadCats(set, names, deathdate) {
  for (var i = 0; i < names.length; i++)
    set[names[i]].death = deathdate;
}
```

catRecord is a separate function for creating these storage objects. It might be useful in other situations, such as creating the object for Spot. *Record* is a term often used for objects like this, which are used to group a limited number of values.

So, let's try to extract the names of the mother cats from the paragraphs like "born 15/11/2003 (mother Spot) ....":

```
function extractMother(paragraph) {
  var start = paragraph.indexOf("(mother ") + "(mother ".length;
  var end = paragraph.indexOf(")");
  return paragraph.slice(start, end);
}
```

```
extractMother("born 15/11/2003 (mother Spot): White Fang");
→ "Spot"
```

Notice how the start position has to be adjusted for the length of "(mother ", because indexOf returns the position of the start of the pattern, not its end.

The new, extended cat algorithm looks like this:

```
function findCats() {
  var cats = {"Spot": catRecord("Spot", new Date(1997, 2, 5), "unknown")};
```

```
function handleParagraph(paragraph) {
  if (startsWith(paragraph, "born"))
    addCats(cats, catNames(paragraph), extractDate(paragraph),
            extractMother(paragraph));
  else if (startsWith(paragraph, "died"))
    deadCats(cats, catNames(paragraph), extractDate(paragraph));
}

for (var mail = 0; mail < ARCHIVE.length; mail++) {
  var paragraphs = ARCHIVE[mail].split("\n");
  for (var i = 0; i < paragraphs.length; i++)
    handleParagraph(paragraphs[i]);
}
return cats;
}
```

For each new cat that is born, we add a record to the cats object. When it dies, this is noted in the record. Thus, the return value of findCats is an object, with each property of that object naming a cat and holding a record with information about that cat.

Data Presentation

Having that extra data allows us to finally have a clue about the cats Aunt Emily talks about. A function like this could be useful:

```
function formatDate(date) {
  return date.getDate() + "/" + (date.getMonth() + 1) + "/" +
    date.getFullYear();
}

function catInfo(data, name) {
  var cat = data[name];
  if (cat == undefined)
    return "No cat by the name of " + name + " is known.";

  var message = name + ", born " + formatDate(cat.birth) +
                " from mother " + cat.mother;
  if ("death" in cat)
    message += ", died " + formatDate(cat.death);
  return message + ".";
}

// For example...
catInfo(catData, "Fat Igor");
→ "Fat Igor, born 1/6/2004 from mother Miss Bushtail."
```

The first return statement in `catInfo` is used as an escape hatch. If there is no data about the given cat, the rest of the function is meaningless, so we immediately return a value, which prevents the rest of the code from running.

In the past, some programmers considered functions that contain multiple return statements sinful. The idea was that this made it hard to see which code was executed and which code was not. Other techniques, which will be discussed in Chapter 4, have made the reasons behind this idea more or less obsolete, but you might still occasionally come across someone who will criticize the use of "shortcut" return statements.

Next, we write a function `oldestCat`, which, given an object containing cats as its argument, returns the name of the oldest living cat:

```
function oldestCat(data) {
  var oldest = null;

  for (var name in data) {
    var cat = data[name];
    if (!("death" in cat) && (oldest == null || oldest.birth > cat.birth))
      oldest = cat;
  }

  if (oldest == null)
    return null;
  else
    return oldest.name;
}
```

The condition in the `if` statement might seem a little intimidating. It can be read as "store the current cat in the variable `oldest` only if it is not dead, and `oldest` is either `null` or a cat that was born after the current cat."

Some More Theory

Now that you are aware of the existence of arrays and objects, I can clarify a few issues that were glossed over before.

The arguments Object

Whenever a function is called, a special "magic" variable named `arguments` is added to the environment in which the function body runs. This variable refers to an object that resembles an array. It has a property 0 for the first argument, 1 for the second, and so on, for every argument the function was given. It also has a `length` property.

However, the arguments object is not a real array—it does not have methods like push, and it does not automatically update its `length` property when you add something to it. This is an unfortunate heritage of the haphazard way in which the language has grown.

```
function argumentCounter() {
  return "You gave me " + arguments.length + " arguments.";
}
argumentCounter("Straw man", "Tautology", "Ad hominem");
→ "You gave me 3 arguments."
```

Some functions can take any number of arguments, like print does. These typically loop over the values in the arguments object to do something with them. Others can take optional arguments that, when not given by the caller, get some sensible default value.

```
function add(number, howmuch) {
  if (arguments.length < 2)
    howmuch = 1;
  return number + howmuch;
}

add(6);
→ 7
add(6, 4);
→ 10
```

We could also extend the range function we made earlier to take a second, optional argument. If only one argument is given, it behaves as earlier and produces a range from 0 to the given number. If two arguments are given, the first indicates the start of the range, and the second indicates the end.

```
function range(start, end) {
  if (arguments.length < 2) {
    end = start;
    start = 0;
  }
  var result = [];
  for (var i = start; i <= end; i++)
    result.push(i);
  return result;
}

range(4);
→ [0, 1, 2, 3, 4]
range(2, 4);
→ [2, 3, 4]
```

This optional argument works a bit differently than the one in the previous example. When it is not given, the first argument takes the role of end, and start becomes 0.

Tying Up a Loose End

You may remember this line of code from the introduction:

```
print(sum(range(1, 10)));
```

We have defined the range operator now. All we need to make this line run is a sum function. This function takes an array of numbers and returns their sum. We can easily write that at this point.

```
function sum(numbers) {
  var total = 0;
  for (var i = 0; i < numbers.length; i++)
    total += numbers[i];
  return total;
}

sum(range(1, 10));
→ 55
```

The Math Object

The previous chapter showed the functions Math.max and Math.min. With what you know now, you will notice that these are really the properties max and min of the object stored under the name Math. This is another role that objects can play: a warehouse holding a number of related values.

There are quite a lot of values inside Math—enough that if they had all been placed directly into the global environment, they would "pollute" it. The more names that have been taken, the more likely one is to accidentally overwrite the value of some variable. For example, it is not a far shot to want to name something max in one of our programs.

Most languages will stop you, or at least warn you, when you are defining a variable with a name that is already taken. JavaScript does neither, so be careful.

In any case, one can find a whole outfit of mathematical functions and constants inside Math. All the trigonometric functions are there—Math.cos, sin, tan, acos, asin, atan. π and e are there, written in all capital letters (Math.PI and Math.E), which is, for historical reasons, a common way to indicate something is a constant value. Math.pow is a good replacement for the power functions we have been writing—it also accepts negative and fractional exponents. Math.sqrt takes square roots. Math.max and Math.min can give the maximum or minimum of two values. Math.round, Math.floor, and Math.ceil will round numbers to the closest whole number, the whole number below it, and the one above it, respectively.

Enumerable Properties

Maybe you already thought of a way to find out what is available in the Math object:

```
for (var name in Math)
  print(name);
```

But alas, nothing appears. Similarly, consider this loop over the properties of an array:

```
for (var name in ["Huey", "Dewey", "Louie"])
  print(name);
```

You will only see 0, 1, and 2, not length, push, or join, which are definitely also in there. It seems some properties of objects are hidden from in loops, or, as this is officially called, *not enumerable*. There is a good reason for this: All objects have a few methods (for example, toString) that convert the object into some kind of relevant string, and you do not want to see those when you are, for example, looking for the cats that you stored in the object.

All properties your programs add to objects are visible. There is no way to make them hidden, which is unfortunate because, as we will see in Chapter 6, it is often useful to be able to add methods to objects without having them show up in our for/in loops.

4

ERROR HANDLING

In most of the example programs so far, I either noted that they expected their input to be valid or ignored the possibility of problematic input altogether. There are situations in which we can get away with this, such as when a program is only for our own use or when we can be positively certain that there will be no unexpected input. In serious programs, however, some kind of disaster plan is usually needed.

Types of Problems

The problematic situations that a program can encounter can roughly be divided into two categories: programmer mistakes and run-time problems. If someone forgets to pass a required argument to a function, that is a programmer mistake. On the other hand, if a program asks the user to enter a name and it gets back an empty string, that is something the programmer cannot prevent.

Programmer Mistakes

The strategy for dealing with programmer mistakes is usually to have the program fail as quickly as possible, preferably in a way that makes it clear what went wrong. If this happens during programming, you can immediately fix the problem. If it happens when a user is using the program, the user should at least be able to tell you something went wrong.

One of the worst things about JavaScript is that it rarely complains. Forgetting an argument is fine; it'll just be given the value undefined. Then using this argument in some numeric computation is also fine; the result will just be NaN. In this way, a mistake often manifests itself only after passing through several functions, or even just results in bogus output.

On the other hand, trying to read a property from an undefined value, or using a function that does not exists, *will* cause an error to be signaled. Our language is not entirely unhelpful.

Thus, when spotting an error-prone situation, one can choose to write some code that explicitly checks the inputs for validity and blows up the program if they are not valid. (We will learn how to blow programs up later in the chapter.) Unfortunately, checking everything will cause the size of your programs to quadruple and will remove any trace of elegance they might have shown. Thus, checking input is always a judgment call—you have to identify the mistakes that are likely to occur and that are likely to have subtle, complicated effects (rather than just causing an error right away).

Most other languages are nicer in this regard—they will signal an error when you try to do something that doesn't make sense, and a lot of them even do *type checking*, where they validate that each operation is performed only on the type of value it operates on, before they even start running the program.

Run-Time Errors

Not all problems can be prevented by the programmer, unfortunately. If your program reads any input at all, or depends on other systems, there is a chance that the input is invalid, or the other systems are broken or unreachable.

Simple programs can afford to just give up when such a problem occurs, but "real" applications are often expected to somehow handle the problem and continue. For example, when asking the user to input a number, we should check the input and, if it is not a number, ask again or tell the user to get lost, but definitely not crash.

Handling Errors

Unexpected input, or some other problematic circumstance, often leads to functions not being able to do what they are supposed to do. Take, for example, this function, between, which extracts the part of a string between two substrings:

```
function between(string, start, end) {
  var startAt = string.indexOf(start) + start.length;
  var endAt = string.indexOf(end, startAt);
  return string.slice(startAt, endAt);
}

between("Louis 'Pops' Armstrong", "'", "'");
→ "Pops"
```

When start or end is not found in the input, what should this function do? It cannot return what it is supposed to return, because the question it was asked doesn't make sense.

Returning a Special Value

When a function encounters a problem that it cannot solve itself, one possible reaction is to return a value that it could not normally return. Since between, in normal operation, will return a string, we could specify it to return undefined (or false, or even 26, but let's not be weirder than we have to be) on bad input.

```
function between(string, start, end) {
  var startAt = string.indexOf(start);
  if (startAt == -1)
    return undefined;
  startAt += start.length;
  var endAt = string.indexOf(end, startAt);
  if (endAt == -1)
    return undefined;

  return string.slice(startAt, endAt);
}
```

You can see that error checking does not generally make functions prettier. But now code that calls between can do something like this:

```
var input = prompt("Tell me something", "");
var parenthesized = between(input, "(", ")");
if (parenthesized != undefined)
  print("You parenthesized '", parenthesized, "'.");
```

In many cases, mostly when errors are likely and the caller should be explicitly checking for them, returning a special value is a perfectly fine way to indicate an error. It does, however, have its downsides. First, what if the function can already return every possible kind of value? For example, consider this function that gets the last element from an array:

```
function lastElement(array) {
  if (array.length > 0)
    return array[array.length - 1];
  else
    return undefined;
}

lastElement([1, 2, undefined]);
→ undefined
```

So, did the array have a last element? Looking at the value `lastElement` returns, it is impossible to say.

The second issue with returning special values is that it can sometimes lead to a whole lot of clutter. If a piece of code calls `between` 10 times, it has to check 10 times whether `undefined` was returned. Also, if a function calls `between` but does not have a strategy to recover from a failure, it will have to check the return value of `between`, and if it is `undefined`, this function can then return `undefined` or some other special value to its caller, which in turn also checks for this value.

Exceptions

When, for some reason, a function cannot return normally, what we actually want is to just stop doing what we are doing and immediately jump back to a place that knows how to handle the problem. That is what *exception handling*—a mechanism present in a lot of modern languages, including JavaScript—does.

The mechanism works like this: It is possible for code to *raise* (or *throw*) an exception, which is a value. Raising an exception somewhat resembles a super-charged return from a function—it does not just jump out of the current function but also out of its callers, all the way up to the top-level call that started the current execution. This is called *unwinding the stack*. You may remember the stack of function calls that was mentioned in Chapter 2. An exception zooms down this stack, throwing away all the call contexts it encounters.

If they always zoomed right down to the base of the stack, exceptions would not be of much use; they would just provide a novel way to blow up your program. Fortunately, it is possible to set obstacles for exceptions along the stack. These *catch* the exception as it is zooming down and can do something with it, after which the program continues running at the point where the exception was caught.

Here's an example:

```
function lastElement(array) {
  if (array.length > 0)
    return array[array.length - 1];
```

```
  else
    throw "Cannot take the last element of an empty array.";
}

function lastElementPlusTen(array) {
  return lastElement(array) + 10;
}

try {
  print(lastElementPlusTen([]));
}
catch (error) {
  print("Something went wrong: ", error);
}
```

throw is the keyword that is used to raise an exception. The keyword try sets up an obstacle for exceptions: When the code in the block after it raises an exception, the catch block will be executed. The variable named in parentheses after the word catch will hold the exception value when this block executes.

Note that the function lastElementPlusTen completely ignores the possibility that lastElement might go wrong. This is the big advantage of exceptions—error-handling code is necessary only at the point where the error occurs and at the point where it is handled. The functions in between can forget all about it.

Well, almost . . .

Cleaning Up After Exceptions

Consider the following situation: A function processThing, wants to make sure that, during its executing, the top-level variable currentThing holds the thing that is being processed. After it finishes processing, it restores this variable to its old value.

```
var currentThing = null;

function processThing(thing) {
  var prevThing = currentThing;
  currentThing = thing;
  /* do complicated processing... */
  currentThing = prevThing;
}
```

What if the complicated processing raises an exception? In that case, the call to processThing will be thrown off the stack by the exception, and currentThing will never be reset to its old value.

try statements can also be followed by a finally keyword, which means "no matter *what* happens, run this code after trying to run the code in the try block." If a function has to clean something up, the cleanup code should usually be put into a finally block:

```
function processThing(thing) {
  var prevThing = currentThing;
  currentThing = thing;
  try {
    /* do complicated processing... */
  }
  finally {
    currentThing = prevThing;
  }
}
```

Now, whether the complicated processing returns normally or throws an exception, currentThing is *always* set back to its old value.

Error Objects

A lot of errors in programs cause the JavaScript environment to raise an exception. For example, this program will print something like Caught: Sasquatch is not defined:

```
try {
  print(Sasquatch);
}
catch (error) {
  print("Caught: " + error.message);
}
```

A special type of objects is raised for problems like this. These always have a message property containing a description of the problem. You can raise similar objects using the new keyword and the Error constructor, giving the message as argument:

```
throw new Error("Wolf!");
```

Unhandled Exceptions

When an exception makes it all the way to the bottom of the stack without being caught, it gets handled by the environment. What this means differs between the different environments. In browsers, sometimes a description of the error is written to some kind of log (reachable in the menu under a name like "JavaScript console" or "error console"); sometimes a window pops up describing the error.

For programmer mistakes or problems that the program cannot possibly handle, just letting the error go through is often okay. An unhandled exception is a reasonable way to signal a broken program, and many JavaScript environments (such as the "debugging" tools included in modern browsers) allow you to inspect these exceptions to see which function calls were on the stack when they occurred, which can be very helpful when trying to find the problem.

Selective Catching

When explicitly handling an exception using catch, one has to be careful not to catch too much. For example, say we have this program:

```
for (;;) {
  try {
    alert(inputNumber() + 5);
    break;
  }
  catch (e) {
    alert("You did not input a number. Try again.");
  }
}
```

The for(;;) construct creates a loop that doesn't terminate on its own. inputNumber is a hypothetical function that asks for a number and raises an exception when invalid input is given. As soon as valid input is given, the try block executes to completion, and the loop will end.

But what if inputNumber raises some other exception? The program will assume that the user is providing invalid input and will loop forever. Thus, it would be wise to verify that the exception raised is indeed caused by invalid input. One way to do this is to raise a special, unique object, like this:

```
var InvalidInputError = new Error("Invalid numeric input");

function inputNumber() {
  var input = Number(prompt("Give me a number", ""));
  if (isNaN(input))
    throw InvalidInputError;
  return input;
}
```

Now we can write our try/catch construct like this:

```
try {
  alert(inputNumber() + 5);
  break;
}
```

```
catch (e) {
  if (e != InvalidInputError)
    throw e;
  alert("You did not input a number. Try again.");
}
```

We check whether the exception raised is the one we are interested in and rethrow it if it is not so that we handle only the problem we're supposed to be handling; we let other kinds of problems go on, either to be caught at another place or to terminate the program if unhandled.

Automated Testing

Because JavaScript programs aren't checked very thoroughly before execution and because manually testing every `if` branch in a big program can take a lot of time, mistakes can sit lurking in the depths of programs, even when they appear to work fine.

For some pieces of code—those that work without too much interaction with their environment—it is very straightforward to write automated tests. These are programs that test programs. To test the `between` function we saw in this chapter, you could, for example, write something like this:

```
function testBetween() {
  function assert(name, x) {
    if (!x)
      throw "Assertion failed: " + name;
  }

  assert("identical delimiters", between("a |b| c", "|", "|") == "b");
  assert("whole string", between("[[n]]", "[[", "]]") == "n");
  assert("reversed", between("]x[", "[", "]") == undefined);
  assert("missing end", between(" -->d ", "-->", "<--") == undefined);
  /* and so on */
}
```

Now, whenever you change `between`, you can run `testBetween` to verify that it still works as intended. Of course, tests for such a simple function feel a bit pointless, but you'll usually be testing bigger, more complex components, where it is not so easy to just "see" that they work.

Writing tests is a lot of work, and keeping them up-to-date when you change your functions is even more work. Thus, whether having a suite of tests is worthwhile is something that has to be decided case by case. Typically, once a piece of code gets sufficiently complex or has many different people working on it, a point is reached where writing, running, and updating the tests becomes less work than testing manually.

There are various pieces of software to make writing and running tests easier. Search the Web for *JavaScript test framework* to read about them.

5

FUNCTIONAL PROGRAMMING

As programs get bigger, they also become more complex and harder to understand. Even the cleverest among us are mere human beings, and a moderate amount of chaos tends to already confuse us. And once confusion sets in, it all goes downhill. Working on something you do not really understand is a bit like cutting random wires on those time-activated bombs they tend to have in movies. If you are lucky, you might get the right one—especially when you're the hero of the movie and strike a suitably dramatic pose—but there is always the possibility of blowing everything up.

Abstraction

Thus, the programmer is always looking for ways to keep the complexity of his programs as low as possible. An important way to do this is to try to make code more *abstract*. When writing a program, it is easy to get sidetracked into small details. You come across some little issue and deal with it, and then you proceed to the next little problem, and so on. This makes the code read like a grandmother's tale.

> Yes, dear, to make pea soup you will need split peas, the dry kind. And you have to soak them at least for a night, or you will have to cook them for hours and hours. I remember one time, when my dull son tried to make pea soup. Would you believe he hadn't soaked the peas? We almost broke our teeth, all of us. Anyway, when you have soaked the peas—and you'll want about a cup of them per person—pay attention because they will expand a bit while they are soaking. If you aren't careful, they will spill out of the pan. Use plenty of water to soak them in. But as I said, use about a cup of them, when they are dry, and after they are soaked, you cook them in four cups of water per cup of dry peas. Let it simmer for two hours, which means you cover it and keep it barely cooking, and then add some diced onions, sliced celery stalk, and maybe a carrot or two and some ham. Let it all cook for a few minutes more, and it is ready to eat.

Another way to write this recipe:

> Per person: 1 cup dried split peas, half a chopped onion, half a carrot, a celery stalk, optionally ham. Soak peas overnight, simmer them for 2 hours in 4 cups of water (per person), add vegetables and ham, and cook for 10 more minutes.

This is shorter, but if you don't know how to soak peas, you'll surely screw up and put them in too little water. But how to soak peas can be looked up, and that is the trick. If you assume a certain basic knowledge in the audience, you can talk in a language that deals with bigger concepts and express things in a much shorter and clearer way. This, more or less, is what abstraction is.

How is this far-fetched recipe story relevant to programming? Well, obviously, the recipe is the program. Furthermore, the basic knowledge that the cook is supposed to have corresponds to the functions and other constructs that are available to the programmer.

If you remember the introduction to this book, constructs such as while make it easier to build loops, and in Chapter 3 we wrote some simple functions to make other functions shorter and more straightforward. Such tools— some of them made available by the language itself; others built by the programmer—are used to reduce the amount of uninteresting details in the rest of the program and thus make that program easier to work with.

Functional programming, the subject of this chapter, creates abstraction through clever ways of combining functions. A programmer armed with a repertoire of fundamental functions and, more importantly, the knowledge of how to use them, is much more effective than one who starts writing every program from scratch. Unfortunately, a standard JavaScript environment comes with deplorably few essential functions, and we have to write them ourselves or make use of somebody else's code (more on that in Chapter 7).

There are other popular approaches to abstraction, most notably object-oriented programming, which is the subject of Chapter 6.

Higher-Order Functions

One ugly detail that, if you have any good taste at all, must be starting to bother you is the endlessly repeated for loop going over an array: for (var i = 0; i < something.length; i++).... Can this be abstracted?

The problem is that, whereas most functions just take some values, combine them, and return something, these for loops contain a piece of code that they must execute. It is easy to write a function that goes over an array and prints out every element:

```
function printArray(array) {
  for (var i = 0; i < array.length; i++)
    print(array[i]);
}
```

But what if we want to do something else than print? Since "doing something" can be represented as a function and since functions are also values, we can pass our action as a function value:

```
function forEach(array, action) {
  for (var i = 0; i < array.length; i++)
    action(array[i]);
}

forEach(["Wampeter", "Foma", "Granfalloon"], print);
```

And by making use of an anonymous function, something just like a for loop can be written with fewer useless details:

```
function sum(numbers) {
  var total = 0;
  forEach(numbers, function (number) {
    total += number;
  });
  return total;
}
```

Note that the variable total is visible inside the anonymous function because of the lexical scoping rules. Also note that this version is hardly shorter than the for loop and requires a rather clunky }); at its end—the brace closes the body of the anonymous function, the parenthesis closes the function call to forEach, and the semicolon is needed because this call is a statement.

You do get a variable bound to the current element in the array, number, so there is no need to use numbers[i] anymore. And when this array is created by evaluating some expression, there is no need to store it in a variable, because it can be passed to forEach directly.

The cat-finding code in Chapter 3 contains a piece like this:

```
var paragraphs = mailArchive[mail].split("\n");
for (var i = 0; i < paragraphs.length; i++)
  handleParagraph(paragraphs[i]);
```

And this can now be written as follows:

```
forEach(mailArchive[mail].split("\n"), handleParagraph);
```

On the whole, using more abstract (or *higher-level*) constructs results in more information and less noise: The code in sum says, "For each number in numbers, add that number to the total," instead of "there is this variable that starts at zero, and it counts upward to the length of the array called numbers, and for every value of this variable we look up the corresponding element in the array and add this to the total. . . ."

What forEach does is take an algorithm, in this case "going over an array," and abstract it. The "gaps" in the algorithm—in this case, what to do for each of these elements—are filled by functions, which are passed to the algorithm function as arguments.

Functions that operate on other functions are called *higher-order functions*. By manipulating functions, they can talk about actions on a new level. The makeAdder function from Chapter 2, which took a number and created a function that added that number to its argument, is also a higher-order function. Instead of taking a function value as an argument, it produces a new function.

Higher-order functions can be used to generalize many algorithms that regular functions cannot easily describe. When you have a repertoire of these functions at your disposal, it can help you think about your code in a clearer way: Instead of a messy set of variables and loops, you can decompose algorithms into a combination of a few fundamental algorithms, which are invoked by name and do not have to be typed out again and again. Being able to write *what* we want to do instead of *how* we do it means we are working at a higher level of abstraction. In practice, this means shorter, clearer, and more pleasant code.

Modifying Functions

Another useful type of higher-order function *modifies* the function value it is given:

```
function negate(func) {
  return function(x) {
    return !func(x);
  };
}
var isNotNaN = negate(isNaN);
isNotNaN(NaN);
→ false
```

The function returned by negate feeds the argument it is given to the original function func and then negates the result.

But what if the function you want to negate takes more than one argument? You can get access to any arguments passed to a function with the arguments pseudo-array, but how do you call a function when you do not know how many arguments you have?

Functions have a method called apply, which is used for situations like this. It takes two arguments. The role of the first argument will be discussed in Chapter 6—for now we'll just pass null. The second argument is an array containing the arguments to which a function must be applied.

```
function negate(func) {
  return function() {
    return !func.apply(null, arguments);
  };
}
```

The reduce Function

The sum function is really a variant of an algorithm that is usually called reduce or fold:

```
function reduce(combine, base, array) {
  forEach(array, function (element) {
    base = combine(base, element);
  });
  return base;
}

function add(a, b) {
  return a + b;
}

function sum(numbers) {
  return reduce(add, 0, numbers);
}
```

reduce combines an array into a single value by repeatedly using a function that combines an element of the array with a base value. This is exactly what sum did, so it can be made shorter by using reduce . . . except that in JavaScript, addition is an operator and not a function, so we had to put it into a function first.

The reason reduce takes the function as its first argument instead of its last, as in forEach, is partly that this is tradition—other languages do it like that—and partly that this allows us to use a trick (partial application) that is discussed later in the chapter. It does mean that, when calling reduce, writing the reducing function as an anonymous function looks a bit weirder, because now the other arguments follow after the function, and the resemblance to a normal for block is lost entirely.

As another example use of reduce, let's write a function that takes an array of numbers as its argument and returns the amount of zeroes that occur in it:

```
function countZeroes(array) {
  function counter(total, element) {
    return total + (element === 0 ? 1 : 0);
  }
  return reduce(counter, 0, array);
}
```

The weird part, with the question mark and the colon, uses a new operator. In Chapter 1 we have seen unary and binary operators. This one is ternary—it acts on three values. Its effect resembles that of if/else, except that, where if conditionally executes statements, this one conditionally chooses expressions. The first part, before the question mark, is the condition. If this condition is true, the expression after the question mark is chosen, 1 in this case. If it is false, the part after the colon, 0 in this case, is chosen.

Use of this operator can make some pieces of code much shorter. When the expressions inside it get very big or when you have to make more decisions inside the conditional parts, just using plain if and else tends to be more readable.

We could also have defined yet another algorithm function, count, and express countZeroes in terms of that:

```
function count(test, array) {
  var counted = 0;
  forEach(array, function(element) {
    if (test(element)) counted++;
  });
  return counted;
}

function countZeroes(array) {
  function isZero(x) {return x === 0;}
  return count(isZero, array);
}
```

Mapping Arrays

Another generally useful "fundamental algorithm" related to arrays is called map. It goes over an array, applying a function to every element, just like forEach. But instead of discarding the values returned by the function, it builds up a new array from these values.

```
function map(func, array) {
  var result = [];
  forEach(array, function (element) {
    result.push(func(element));
  });
  return result;
}

map(Math.round, [0.01, 2, 9.89, Math.PI]);
→ [0, 2, 10, 3]
```

Note that the first argument is called func, not function, which is because function is a keyword and thus not a valid variable name.

The Sad Story of the Recluse

There once was, living in the deep mountain forests of the Western Netherlands, a recluse. Most of the time, he just wandered around his mountain, talking to trees and laughing with birds. But now and then, when the pouring rain trapped him in his little hut and the howling wind made him feel unbearably small, the recluse felt an urge to write something. He wanted to pour some thoughts out onto paper, where they could maybe grow bigger than he himself was.

After failing miserably at poetry, fiction, and philosophy, the recluse finally decided to write a technical book. In his youth, he had done some computer programming, and he figured that if he could just write a good book about that, fame and recognition would follow.

So he wrote. At first he wrote on fragments of tree bark, but that soon became a little too hard-core for him. So, he went down to the nearest village and bought himself a laptop computer. After a few chapters, he realized he wanted to put the book in HTML format in order to put it on his website.

HTML

Are you familiar with HTML? It is the method used to format pages on the Web, and we will be using it a few times in this book, so it would be nice if you know how it works, at least generally. If you are a good student, you could go search the Web for a good introduction to HTML now and come back here when you have read it. Most of you probably are lousy students, so I will just give a short explanation right here and hope that is enough.

HTML stands for HyperText Markup Language. An HTML document is all text. Because it must be able to express the structure of this text, such as information about which text is a heading, which text should be purple, and so on, a few characters have a special meaning, somewhat like backslashes in JavaScript strings. The "less-than" and "greater-than" characters are used to create *tags*. A tag gives extra information about the text in the document. It can stand on its own, for example to mark the place where a picture should appear in the page, or it can contain text and other tags, for example when it marks the start and end of a paragraph.

Some tags are compulsory. For example, a whole HTML document must always be wrapped between `<html>` and `</html>`. Here is an example of an HTML document:

```
<html>
  <head>
    <title>A quote</title>
  </head>
  <body>
    <h1>A quote</h1>
    <blockquote>
      <p>The connection between the language in which we
      think/program and the problems and solutions we can imagine
      is very close.  For this reason restricting language
      features with the intent of eliminating programmer errors is
      at best dangerous.</p>
      <p>-- Bjarne Stroustrup</p>
    </blockquote>
    <p>Also, here is a picture of an ostrich:</p>
    <img src="img/ostrich.png">
  </body>
</html>
```

Elements that contain text or other tags are first opened with `<tagname>` and afterward finished with `</tagname>`. The `html` element always contains two children: `head` and `body`. The first contains information *about* the document; the second contains the actual document.

Most tag names are cryptic abbreviations. `h1` stands for "heading 1," heading used at the top level of a document. There are also `h2` to `h6` for successively more minor headings. `p` means "paragraph," and `img` stands for "image." The `img` element does not contain any text or other tags, but it does have some extra information, `src="img/ostrich.png"`, which is called an *attribute*. In this case, it contains information about the image file that should be shown here.

Because `<` and `>` have a special meaning in HTML documents, they cannot be written directly in the text of the document. If you want to say `5 < 10` in an HTML document, you have to write `5 &lt; 10`, where `lt` stands for "less than." `&gt;` is used for `>`. Because these codes also give the ampersand character a special meaning, a plain `&` is written as `&amp;`.

Now, those are only the bare basics of HTML, but they should be enough to make it through this chapter—and later chapters that deal with HTML documents—without getting entirely confused.

The Recluse's Text File

Picking up the story again, the recluse wanted to have his book in HTML format. At first he just wrote all the tags directly into his manuscript, but typing all those less-than and greater-than signs made his fingers hurt, and he constantly forgot to write & when he needed an &. It cramped his style.

The solution that he came up with was this: He would write the book as plain text, following some simple rules about the way paragraphs were separated and the way headings looked. Then, he would write a program to convert this text into precisely the HTML that he wanted.

The rules are these:

1. Paragraphs are separated by blank lines.

2. A paragraph that starts with a % symbol is a heading. The more % symbols, the smaller the heading.

3. Inside paragraphs, pieces of text can be emphasized by putting them between asterisks.

4. Footnotes are written between braces.

After he had struggled painfully with his book for six months, the recluse had finished only a few paragraphs. At this point his hut was struck by lightning, which killed him and forever put his writing ambitions to rest. From the charred remains of his laptop, I managed to recover the following file:

```
% The Book of Programming

%% The Two Aspects

Below the surface of the machine, the program moves. Without effort,
it expands and contracts. In great harmony, electrons scatter and
regroup. The forms on the monitor are but ripples on the water. The
essence stays invisibly below.

When the creators built the machine, they put in the processor and the
memory. From these arise the two aspects of the program.

The aspect of the processor is the active substance. It is called
Control. The aspect of the memory is the passive substance. It is
called Data.

Data is made of merely bits, yet it takes complex forms. Control
consists only of simple instructions, yet it performs difficult
tasks. From the small and trivial, the large and complex arise.

The program source is Data. Control arises from it. The Control
proceeds to create new Data. The one is born from the other, the
other is useless without the one. This is the harmonious cycle of
Data and Control.
```

Of themselves, Data and Control are without structure. The programmers of old molded their programs out of this raw substance. Over time, the amorphous Data has crystallized into data types, and the chaotic Control was wrung into control structures and functions.

%% Short Sayings

When a student asked Fu-Tzu about the nature of the cycle of Data and Control, Fu-Tzu replied 'Think of a compiler, compiling itself.'

A student asked, 'The programmers of old used only simple machines and no programming languages, yet they made beautiful programs. Why do we use complicated machines and programming languages?' Fu-Tzu replied 'The builders of old used only sticks and clay, yet they made beautiful huts.'

A hermit spent 10 years writing a program. 'My program can compute the motion of the stars on a 286-computer running MS DOS,' he proudly announced. 'Nobody owns a 286-computer or uses MS DOS anymore,' Fu-Tzu responded.

Fu-Tzu had written a small program that was full of global state and dubious shortcuts. Reading it, a student asked 'You warned us against these techniques, yet I find them in your program. How can this be?' Fu-Tzu said, 'There is no need to fetch a water hose when the house is not on fire.'{This is not to be read as an encouragement of sloppy programming, but rather as a warning against neurotic adherence to rules of thumb.}

%% Wisdom

A student was complaining about digital numbers. 'When I take the root of two and then square it again, the result is already inaccurate!' Overhearing him, Fu-Tzu laughed. 'Here is a sheet of paper. Write down the precise value of the square root of two for me.'

Fu-Tzu said, 'When you cut against the grain of the wood, much strength is needed. When you program against the grain of a problem, much code is needed.'

Tzu-li and Tzu-ssu were boasting about the size of their latest programs. 'Two-hundred thousand lines,' said Tzu-li, 'not counting comments!' Tzu-ssu responded, 'Psah, mine is almost a *million* lines already.' Fu-Tzu said, 'My best program has five hundred lines.' Hearing this, Tzu-li and Tzu-ssu were enlightened.

A student had been sitting motionless behind his computer for hours, frowning darkly. He was trying to write a beautiful solution to a difficult problem but could not find the right approach. Fu-Tzu hit him on the back of his head and shouted, '*Type something!*' The student started writing an ugly solution. After he had finished, he suddenly understood the beautiful solution.

%% Progression

A beginning programmer writes his programs like an ant builds her hill, one piece at a time, without thought for the bigger structure. His programs will be like loose sand. They may stand for a while, but growing too big they fall apart{Referring to the danger of internal inconsistency and duplicated structure in unorganized code.}.

Realizing this problem, the programmer will start to spend a lot of time thinking about structure. His programs will be rigidly structured, like rock sculptures. They are solid, but when they must change, violence must be done to them{Referring to the fact that structure tends to put restrictions on the evolution of a program.}.

The master programmer knows when to apply structure and when to leave things in their simple form. His programs are like clay, solid yet malleable.

To honor the memory of our good recluse, I would like to finish his HTML-generating program for him. A good approach to this problem goes like this:

1. Split the file into paragraphs by cutting it at every empty line.
2. Remove the % characters from heading paragraphs and mark them as headings.
3. Process the text of the paragraphs themselves, splitting them into normal parts, emphasized parts, and footnotes.
4. Move all the footnotes to the bottom of the document, leaving numbers in their place.
5. Wrap each piece into the correct HTML tags.
6. Combine everything into a single HTML document.

This approach does not allow footnotes inside emphasized text, or vice versa. This is kind of arbitrary but helps keep the example code simple. If, at the end of the chapter, you feel like an extra challenge, you can try to revise the program to support "nested" markup.

Finding Paragraphs

Step 1 of the algorithm is trivial. A blank line is what you get when you have two newlines in a row, and if you remember the split method that strings have, which we saw in Chapter 3, you will realize that this will do the trick:

```
var paragraphs = RECLUSEFILE.split("\n\n");
paragraphs.length;
→ 22
```

To separate heading paragraphs from normal ones, this function can be used:

```
function processParagraph(paragraph) {
  var heading = 0;
  while (paragraph.charAt(heading) == "%")
    heading++;
  if (heading > 0)
    return {type: "h" + heading, content: paragraph.slice(heading + 1)};
  else
    return {type: "p", content: paragraph};
}

processParagraph(paragraphs[0]);
→ {type: "h1", content: "The Book of Programming"}
```

This function creates an object, whose type property indicates the kind of HTML tag this paragraph must be wrapped in and whose content property contains the actual text in the paragraph.

We could now try the map function we wrote earlier to conveniently convert all the paragraphs in the document:

```
map(processParagraph, RECLUSEFILE.split("\n\n"));
→ [{type: "h1", content: "The Book of Programming"}, /* etc */]
```

Emphasis and Footnotes

We are getting ahead of ourselves, though; we forgot step 3 of the algorithm:

> Process the text of the paragraphs themselves, splitting them into normal parts, emphasized parts, and footnotes.

This can be decomposed into the following:

1. If the paragraph starts with an asterisk, take off the emphasized part and store it.

2. If the paragraph starts with an opening brace, take off the footnote and store it.

3. Otherwise, take off the part until the first emphasized part or footnote, or until the end of the string, and store it as normal text.

4. If there is anything left in the paragraph, start at step 1 again.

To implement this, we can write something like the following function. It uses the concat method on arrays, which creates a new array that concatenates the argument it is given with the array on which it is called. Also remember that indexOf returns -1 when it doesn't find its substring.

```
function splitParagraph(text) {
  function split(pos) {
    if (pos == text.length) {
      return [];
    }
    else if (text.charAt(pos) == "*") {
      var end = findClosing("*", pos + 1),
          frag = {type: "emphasized", content: text.slice(pos + 1, end)};
      return [frag].concat(split(end + 1));
    }
    else if (text.charAt(pos) == "{") {
      var end = findClosing("}", pos + 1),
          frag = {type: "footnote", content: text.slice(pos + 1, end)};
      return [frag].concat(split(end + 1));
    }
    else {
      var end = findOpeningOrEnd(pos),
          frag = {type: "normal", content: text.slice(pos, end)};
      return [frag].concat(split(end));
    }
  }

  function findClosing(character, from) {
    var end = text.indexOf(character, from);
    if (end == -1) throw new Error("Missing closing '" + character + "'");
    else return end;
  }

  function findOpeningOrEnd(from) {
    function indexOrEnd(character) {
      var index = text.indexOf(character, from);
      return index == -1 ? text.length : index;
    }
    return Math.min(indexOrEnd("*"), indexOrEnd("{"));
  }

  return split(0);
}
```

Take a moment to see how this works. The split function is given a position in the string from which to start and creates an array of fragment objects for the rest of the string. It does that by looking at the character at the given position, creating a single fragment if possible, and then calling itself again to handle the part of the string after that fragment. If the position given is the end of the string, it can just return an empty array.

The two other internal functions are used to find the end of a fragment. findClosing looks for a character that closes the fragment, raising an error when it can't find it, and findOpeningOrEnd sees whether it can find a character that starts a "special" fragment, returning the end of the string when it can't find any.

This function is written in a particular style—it uses recursion rather than loops and *never* modifies any values or variable bindings. This is a style of programming that tends to produce nicely succinct programs that are easy to reason about. In some other programming languages, those called *functional languages*, this is how typical programs look. However, JavaScript is not very well suited for this style (recursion is slow and might overflow the stack, and calling concat like this is wasteful, because it creates a whole new array every time), so we have to compromise. This replacement for the split function in the example is more typical JavaScript code and will be more efficient:

```
function split() {
  var pos = 0, fragments = [];
  while (pos < text.length) {
    if (text.charAt(pos) == "*") {
      var end = findClosing("*", pos + 1);
      fragments.push({type: "emphasized", content: text.slice(pos + 1, end)});
      pos = end + 1;
    }
    else if (text.charAt(pos) == "{") {
      var end = findClosing("}", pos + 1);
      fragments.push({type: "footnote", content: text.slice(pos + 1, end)});
      pos = end + 1;
    }
    else {
      var end = findOpeningOrEnd(pos);
      fragments.push({type: "normal", content: text.slice(pos, end)});
      pos = end;
    }
  }
  return fragments;
}
```

Basically, the recursive calls have been replaced by a while loop, and the fragment array is no longer built by concatenating subparts, but explicitly modified by pushing in new elements. Because the fragments value and the pos variable are now being modified, it is a little harder to track the way data flows—it no longer goes in just one direction (being created and then used) as in the first version of the function.

We can now wire processParagraph to also split the text inside the paragraphs before it returns them (only the return lines were changed):

```
function processParagraph(paragraph) {
  var heading = 0;
  while (paragraph.charAt(heading) == "%")
    heading++;
  if (heading > 0)
    return {type: "h" + heading, content: splitParagraph(paragraph.slice(heading
      + 1))};
  else
    return {type: "p", content: splitParagraph(paragraph)};
}
```

Moving the Footnotes

Mapping processParagraph over the array of paragraphs gives us an array of paragraph objects, which in turn contain arrays of fragment objects. The next thing to do is to take out the footnotes, which we want to show at the bottom of the page, and put references to them in their place. Something like this:

```
function extractFootnotes(paragraphs) {
  var footnotes = [];
  var currentNote = 0;

  function replaceFootnote(fragment) {
    if (fragment.type == "footnote") {
      currentNote++;
      footnotes.push(fragment);
      fragment.number = currentNote;
      return {type: "reference", number: currentNote};
    }
    else {
      return fragment;
    }
  }

  forEach(paragraphs, function(paragraph) {
    paragraph.content = map(replaceFootnote, paragraph.content);
  });

  return footnotes;
}
```

The `replaceFootnote` function is called on every fragment. When it gets a fragment that should stay where it is, it just returns it, but when it gets a footnote, it stores this footnote in the `footnotes` array and returns a reference to it instead. In the process, every footnote and reference are also numbered.

Note that this function *modifies* the paragraph objects in the array it is passed.

Generating HTML

That gives us enough tools to extract the information we need from the file. All that is left now is generating the correct HTML.

A lot of people think that concatenating strings is a great way to produce HTML. When they need a link to, for example, a site where you can play the game of Go, they will write the following:

```
var url = "http://www.gokgs.com/";
var text = "Play Go!";
var linkText = "<a href=\"" + url + "\">" + text + "</a>";
```

(a is the tag used to create links in HTML documents.) Not only is this clumsy, but when the string text happens to include an angular bracket or an ampersand, it is also wrong—an angular bracket would be interpreted as the start of a tag, which usually prevents the text after it from being displayed by the browser.

The trick with HTML generation is to treat your document as a data structure instead of a flat piece of text. JavaScript's objects provide a very easy way to model this:

```
var linkObject = {name: "a",
                  attributes: {href: "http://www.gokgs.com/"},
                  content: ["Play Go!"]};
```

Each HTML element contains a `name` property, giving the name of the tag it represents. When it has attributes, it also contains an `attributes` property, which contains an object in which the attributes are stored. When it has content, there is a `content` property, containing an array of other elements contained in this element. Strings play the role of pieces of text in our HTML document, so the array `["Play Go!"]` means that this link has only one element inside it, which is a simple piece of text.

Typing in these objects directly is clumsy, but we don't have to do that. We provide a shortcut function to do this for us:

```
function tag(name, content, attributes) {
  return {name: name, attributes: attributes, content: content};
}
```

Note that, since we allow the attributes and content of an element to be undefined if they are not applicable, the second and third arguments to this function can be left off when they are not needed.

tag is still rather primitive, so we write shortcuts for common types of elements, such as links, or the outer structure of a simple document:

```
function link(target, text) {
  return tag("a", [text], {href: target});
}

function htmlDoc(title, bodyContent) {
  return tag("html", [tag("head", [tag("title", [title])]),
                      tag("body", bodyContent)]);
}
```

When we have created a document as a set of objects, it will have to be reduced to a string. Building this string from such data structures is very straightforward. The hardest part is transforming the special characters in the text of our document:

```
function escapeHTML(text) {
  var replacements = [[/&/g, "&amp;"], [/"/g, "&quot;"],
                     [/</g, "&lt;"], [/>/g, "&gt;"]];
  forEach(replacements, function(replace) {
    text = text.replace(replace[0], replace[1]);
  });
  return text;
}
```

The replace method of strings creates a new string in which all occurrences of the pattern in the first argument are replaced by the second argument, so "Borobudur".replace(/r/g, "k") gives "Bokobuduk". Don't worry about the pattern syntax here—we'll get to that in Chapter 8. The escapeHTML function puts the different replacements that have to be made into an array so that it can loop over them and apply them to the argument one by one.

Double quotes are also replaced, because we will also be using this function for the text inside the attributes of HTML tags. Those will be surrounded by double quotes and thus must not have any double quotes inside of them.

Calling replace four times means the computer has to go over the whole string four times to check and replace its content. This is not very efficient. If we cared enough, we could write a more complex version of this function, something that resembles the splitParagraph function we saw earlier, to go over it only once. For now, we are too lazy for this. Chapter 8, again, shows a much better way to do this.

The next helper function takes an attribute object and turns it into a string, for example {src: "picture.png", alt: "The Picture"} becomes " src=\"picture.png\" alt=\"The Picture\"".

```
function renderAttributes(attributes) {
  if (attributes == null) return "";

  var result = [];
  for (var name in attributes)
    result.push(" " + name + "=\"" + escapeHTML(attributes[name]) + "\"");
  return result.join("");
}
```

To turn an HTML element object into a string, we can use a recursive inner function like this:

```
function renderHTML(element) {
  var pieces = [];

  function render(element) {
    // Text node
    if (typeof element == "string") {
      pieces.push(escapeHTML(element));
    }
    // Empty tag
    else if (!element.content || element.content.length == 0) {
      pieces.push("<" + element.name +
                  renderAttributes(element.attributes) + ">");
    }
    // Tag with content
    else {
      pieces.push("<" + element.name +
                  renderAttributes(element.attributes) + ">");
      forEach(element.content, render);
      pieces.push("</" + element.name + ">");
    }
  }

  render(element);
  return pieces.join("");
}
```

Why am I using arrays to accumulate strings and then calling join on them, instead of just starting with an empty string and adding content with the += operator?

It turns out that creating new strings, especially big strings, is quite a bit of work for the computer. Remember that JavaScript string values never change. If you concatenate something to them, a new string is created, and the old ones stay intact. If we build up a big string by concatenating lots of little strings, new strings have to be created at every step, only to be thrown away when the next piece is concatenated to them. If, on the other hand, we store all the little strings in an array and then join them, only *one* big string has to be created.

Trying out our HTML-generating system, it seems to work:

```
renderHTML(link("http://www.nedroid.com", "Drawings!"));
→ "<a href=\"http://www.nedroid.com\">Drawings!</a>"
```

Now, I should probably warn you that this program is not quite finished. Some HTML tags *have* to be closed, even if they do not contain content. Our generator doesn't know about such tags and thus could output invalid HTML if such tags are specified without a content array. In this chapter, we put content inside of each tag that needs a closing tag, so this shortcoming doesn't cause problems.

Converting the Recluse's Book

Armed with our HTML generator, we can render the book. We'll start with a function renderFragment that takes a fragment (normal text, emphasized text, or footnote reference) and converts it to an HTML object:

```
function renderFragment(fragment) {
  if (fragment.type == "reference")
    return tag("sup", [link("#footnote" + fragment.number,
                            String(fragment.number))]);
  else if (fragment.type == "emphasised")
    return tag("em", [fragment.content]);
  else if (fragment.type == "normal")
    return fragment.content;
}
```

A sup tag will show its content as "superscript," which means it will be smaller and aligned a little higher than normal text. The target of the link will be something like "#footnote1". Links that contain a # character refer to "anchors" within a page, and in this case we will use them to have the footnote link take the reader to the bottom of the page, where the footnotes live.

The tag to render emphasized fragments with is em. Note how the second argument to the tag function must be wrapped in [and]—the content of an element is specified to be an *array* of other elements, even if there is only one of them.

Rendering a whole paragraph is very easy now. Remember that we already determined the HTML tag the paragraphs should be wrapped in and put that in their type property.

```
function renderParagraph(paragraph) {
  return tag(paragraph.type, map(renderFragment, paragraph.content));
}
```

We are almost finished. The only thing that we do not have a rendering function for yet are the footnotes. To make the "#footnote1" links work, an anchor must be included with every footnote. In HTML, anchors are created with the a tag, just like links. To make it an anchor instead of a link, the tag gets a name attribute, rather than of an href attribute.

```
function renderFootnote(footnote) {
  var anchor = tag("a", [], {name: "footnote" + footnote.number});
  var number = "[" + footnote.number + "] ";
  return tag("p", [tag("small", [anchor, number, footnote.content])]);
}
```

Now footnotes come out as paragraphs that start with the (hidden, used only for linking) anchor, followed by the number of the note, for example "[1]", followed by the text of the footnote.

Finally, then, here is the function that, when given a file in the correct format and a document title, returns an HTML document:

```
function renderFile(file, title) {
  var paragraphs = map(processParagraph, file.split("\n\n"));
  var footnotes = map(renderFootnote, extractFootnotes(paragraphs));
  var body = map(renderParagraph, paragraphs).concat(footnotes);
  return renderHTML(htmlDoc(title, body));
}
```

Calling renderFile(RECLUSEFILE, "The Book of Programming")); will now give us a big HTML document, which contains a nicely formatted version of the recluse's book.

Other Functional Tricks

Before moving on to the next chapter, I would like to show you a few more functional techniques that can, once you've gotten used to them, make your programs more succinct.

Operator Functions

When using higher-order functions, it is often annoying that operators are not functions in JavaScript. For example, we had to define the add function earlier in this chapter. Writing these out every time we need them is a pain. One way to get around that is to create an object like this:

```
var op = {
  "+": function(a, b){return a + b;},
  "==": function(a, b){return a == b;},
  "===": function(a, b){return a === b;},
  "!": function(a){return !a;}
```

```
/* and so on */
};
```

So, we can write reduce(op["+"], 0, [1, 2, 3, 4, 5]) to sum an array.

Partial Application

But what if we need a function where one of the operator's arguments is already given? For example, say we need a function that compares its argument to 0 or adds 1 to its argument. We would still need to write a new function. For cases like that, something called *partial application* is useful. We want to take a function X and one or more arguments and then create a new function that calls X with both the original arguments and any newly passed ones.

For example, partial(op["*"], 5) should return a new function that multiplies its argument by five. We can define partial by making creative use of the apply method of a function:

```
function partial(func) {
  var knownArgs = arguments;
  return function() {
    var realArgs = [];
    for (var i = 1; i < knownArgs.length; i++)
      realArgs.push(knownArgs[i]);
    for (var i = 0; i < arguments.length; i++)
      realArgs.push(arguments[i]);
    return func.apply(null, realArgs);
  };
}
```

The building of the argument array could have been much more elegant if arguments held a real array (knownArgs.slice(1).concat(arguments)), but alas, they are pseudo-arrays on which the concat method does not work. To work around this, we copy them "manually." The first loop starts at 1, because the first element to the outer function is the function to wrap, not one of the arguments that must be passed to it.

The variable knownArgs is necessary because, inside the inner function, the arguments variable refers to the inner function's arguments, not the arguments of partial.

Now, a function that tests whether its argument is ten can be written as partial(op["=="], 10). All elements in an array can be incremented like this:

```
map(partial(op["+"], 1), [0, 2, 4, 6, 8, 10]);
→ [1, 3, 5, 7, 9, 11]
```

The reason map takes its function argument before its array argument is that it is often useful to partially apply map by giving it a function. This "lifts" the function from operating on a single value to operating on an array of values. For example, if you have an array of arrays of numbers, and you want to square them all, you do this:

```
function square(x) {return x * x;}
```

```
map(partial(map, square), [[10], [0, 1], [3]]);
→ [[100], [0, 1], [9]]
```

Furthermore, the sum function can now simply be written like this:

```
var sum = partial(reduce, op["+"], 0);
```

Composition

One last trick that can be useful when juggling function values is *function composition*. At the start of this chapter I showed a function negate, which applies the Boolean *not* operator to the result of calling a function:

```
function negate(func) {
  return function() {
    return !func.apply(null, arguments);
  };
}
```

This is a special case of a general pattern: Call function A, and then apply function B to the result. Compositions is a common concept in mathematics. It can be expressed as a higher-order function like this:

```
function compose(f1, f2) {
  return function() {
    return f1(f2.apply(null, arguments));
  };
}
```

Here's an example:

```
var isNotNaN = compose(op["!"], isNaN);
isNotNaN(5);
→ true
```

Here we defined a new function without using the function keyword at all. Because such definitions are typically shorter, they are great when you want to create a simple function to give to, for example map or reduce.

Functions defined like this tend to be a little slower, because they add more indirect function calls. Most of the time, this is not an issue, since most code will be executed less than once a second, and a few extra microseconds spent won't be noticed. But for functions that you end up calling thousands of times per second, you should consider just writing the function out directly.

6

OBJECT-ORIENTED PROGRAMMING

In the early 1990s, a thing called *object-oriented programming* swept through the software industry. It defined a whole new paradigm for writing programs. A bunch of ideas that had been simmering in research labs, and obscure experimental programming languages for a decade were finally picked up by the mainstream. Books were being written, courses were being given, and a whole culture sprang up. We had found *the right way to write programs.*

As it usually goes with new fashions, the effectiveness of this new style of programming was greatly exaggerated. It turns out that programming was still hard, even with objects. In fact, some of the rigidly object-oriented ideas that were adopted (and enforced) by languages like Java probably do more harm than good.

Regardless, the central techniques to come out of object-oriented programming are very effective and worth learning. In this chapter, we will discuss these ideas, along with JavaScript's (rather eccentric) take on them.

Objects

As the name suggests, object-oriented programming is related to objects. So far, we have used objects as loose aggregations of values, adding and altering their properties whenever we saw fit. In an object-oriented approach, objects are viewed as little worlds of their own, and the outside world may touch them only through a limited and well-defined interface, which consists of a number of specific methods and properties.

The Date and Error objects we have seen also work like this. Instead of providing regular functions for working with the objects, they provide a way to create such objects, using the new keyword, and a number of methods and properties that provide the rest of the interface.

Defining Methods

One way to give an object methods is to simply attach function values to it, as in the following code:

```
var rabbit = {};
rabbit.speak = function(line) {
  print("The rabbit says '", line, "'");
};

rabbit.speak("I'm alive.");
```

In most cases, the method will also need to know *who* it should act on. For example, if there are different rabbits, the speak method must indicate which rabbit is speaking. For this purpose, there is a special variable called this. When the function is called as a method (meaning it is looked up as a property and immediately called, as in object.method()), this will point to the relevant object.

```
function speak(line) {
  print("The ", this.adjective, " rabbit says '", line, "'");
}
var whiteRabbit = {adjective: "white", speak: speak};
var fatRabbit = {adjective: "fat", speak: speak};

whiteRabbit.speak("Oh my ears and whiskers, how late it's getting!");
fatRabbit.speak("I could sure use a carrot right now.");
```

The previous code uses the this variable to insert the type of rabbit that is speaking into the output text. It will print the following:

```
The white rabbit says 'Oh my ears and whiskers, how late it's getting!'
The fat rabbit says 'I could sure use a carrot right now.'
```

I can now clarify the mysterious first argument to the `apply` method, for which we always used `null` in Chapter 5. This argument can be used to specify the object that the function must be applied to. (For nonmethod functions, this is irrelevant, which is the reason for the `null`.) We could also call speak on the fat rabbit like this:

```
speak.apply(fatRabbit, ["Yum."]);
```

Functions also have a `call` method, which is similar to `apply`, but you can give the arguments for the function separately instead of as an array:

```
speak.call(fatRabbit, "Burp.");
```

For functions with more than one argument, using `call` and `apply` looks like this:

```
function run(from, to) {
  print("The ", this.adjective, " rabbit runs from ", from, " to ", to, ".");
}
run.apply(whiteRabbit, ["A", "B"]);
run.call(fatRabbit, "the cupboard", "the fridge");
```

Constructors

The `new` keyword provides a convenient way of creating new objects. When a function is called with the operator `new` in front of it, its `this` variable will point at a *new* object, which it will automatically return (unless it explicitly returns something else using return). Functions used to create new objects like this are called *constructors*. Here is a constructor for rabbits:

```
function Rabbit(adjective) {
  this.adjective = adjective;
  this.speak = function(line) {
    print("The ", this.adjective, " rabbit says '", line, "'");
  };
}

var killerRabbit = new Rabbit("killer");
killerRabbit.speak("GRAAAAAAAAAH!");
```

It is convention to start the names of constructors with a capital letter. This makes it easy to distinguish them from other functions. The language does not enforce this, but it is good practice to follow it.

Building from Prototype

Why is the new keyword even necessary? After all, we could have simply written this:

```
function makeRabbit(adjective) {
  return {
    adjective: adjective,
    speak: function(line) {/*etc*/}
  };
}

var blackRabbit = makeRabbit("black");
```

But that is not entirely the same. new does a few things behind the scenes. For one thing, our killerRabbit has a property called constructor, which points at the Rabbit function that created it. blackRabbit also has such a property, but it points at the Object function.

Where did this constructor property come from? It is part of the prototype of a rabbit. Prototypes are a powerful, if somewhat confusing, part of the way JavaScript objects work. Every object is based on a prototype, which gives it a set of inherent properties. The simple objects we have used so far are based on the most basic prototype, which is associated with the Object constructor, and are thus shared by all objects. (Typing {}, by the way, is equivalent to typing new Object().)

toString is a method that is part of the Object prototype. This means that all simple objects have a toString method, which converts them to a string. In fact, every object has a toString method, since even if an object has another prototype, that prototype is itself an object, which will (directly or indirectly) be based on the Object prototype.

Constructors and Prototypes

Our rabbit objects are based on the prototype associated with the Rabbit constructor. You can use a constructor's prototype property to access this prototype.

Every function you define automatically gets a prototype property, which holds an object—the prototype of the function. This prototype gets a constructor property, which points back at the function to which it belongs. Because the rabbit prototype is itself an object, it is based on the Object prototype and shares its toString method. Thus, any rabbit created with the Rabbit constructor has this method.

Even though objects seem to share the properties of their prototype, this sharing is one-way. The properties of the prototype influence the object based on it, and changes to these objects never affect the prototype.

The precise rules are these: When looking up the value of a property, JavaScript first looks at the properties that the object *itself* has. If there is a property that has the name we are looking for, that is the value we get. If there is no such property, it continues searching the prototype of the object, and then the prototype of the prototype, and so on. If no property is found, the value undefined is given. On the other hand, when *setting* the value of a property, JavaScript never goes to the prototype but always sets the property in the object itself. This means you can "override" properties in your own objects to give them more specific, appropriate values than the generic ones it takes from its prototype. The following code demonstrates this technique:

```
Rabbit.prototype.teeth = "small";
killerRabbit.teeth;
→ "small"
killerRabbit.teeth = "long, sharp, and bloody";
killerRabbit.teeth;
→ "long, sharp, and bloody"
Rabbit.prototype.teeth;
→ "small"
```

The following diagram sketches the situation after this code has run. The Rabbit and Object prototypes lie behind killerRabbit as a kind of backdrop, where properties that are not found in the object itself can be looked up.

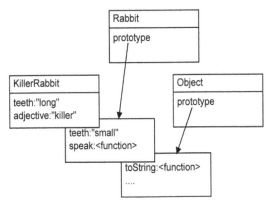

This does mean that the prototype can be used at any time to add new properties and methods to all objects based on it. For example, it might become necessary for our rabbits to dance.

```
Rabbit.prototype.dance = function() {
  print("The ", this.adjective, " rabbit dances a jig.");
};
```

And, as you might have guessed, the prototypical rabbit is the perfect place for those values that all rabbits have in common, such as the speak method. Here is a new approach to the Rabbit constructor:

```
function Rabbit(adjective) {
  this.adjective = adjective;
}
Rabbit.prototype.speak = function(line) {
  print("The ", this.adjective, " rabbit says '", line, "'");
};
```

Prototype Pollution

The fact that all objects have a prototype and receive some properties from this prototype can be tricky. It means that using an object to store a set of things, such as the cats from Chapter 3, can go wrong. If, for example, we wondered whether there is a cat called "constructor", we would have checked it like this:

```
var noCatsAtAll = {};
if ("constructor" in noCatsAtAll)
  print("Yes, there definitely is a cat called 'constructor'.");
```

This is problematic. A related issue is that it can often be useful to extend the prototypes of standard constructors such as Object and Array with new useful functions. For example, we could give all objects a method called properties, which returns an array with the names of the (nonhidden) properties that the object has:

```
Object.prototype.properties = function() {
  var result = [];
  for (var property in this)
    result.push(property);
  return result;
};

var test = {x: 10, y: 3};
test.properties();
→ ["x", "y", "properties"]
```

And that immediately shows the problem. Now that the Object prototype has a property called properties, looping over the properties of any object, using for and in, will also give us that shared property, which is generally not what we want. We are interested only in the properties that the object itself has.

Fortunately, there is a way to find out whether a property belongs to the object itself or to one of its prototypes. Unfortunately, it does make looping over the properties of an object a bit clumsier. Every object has a method called hasOwnProperty, which tells us whether the object has a property with a given name. Using this, we could rewrite our properties method like this:

```
Object.prototype.properties = function() {
  var result = [];
  for (var property in this) {
    if (this.hasOwnProperty(property))
      result.push(property);
  }
  return result;
};

var test = {"Fat Igor": true, "Fireball": true};
test.properties();
→ ["Fat Igor", "Fireball"]
```

And of course, we can abstract that into a higher-order function. Note that the action function is called with both the name of the property and the value it has in the object.

```
function forEachIn(object, action) {
  for (var property in object) {
    if (object.hasOwnProperty(property))
      action(property, object[property]);
  }
}
```

But, what if we find a cat named hasOwnProperty? (You never know.) It will be stored in the object, and the next time we want to go over the collection of cats, calling object.hasOwnProperty will fail, because that property no longer points at a function value. This can be solved by doing something even uglier:

```
function forEachIn(object, action) {
  for (var property in object) {
    if (Object.prototype.hasOwnProperty.call(object, property))
      action(property, object[property]);
  }
}
```

Here, instead of using the method found in the object itself, we get the method from the Object prototype and then use call to apply it to the right object. Unless someone actually messes with the method in Object.prototype (don't *ever* do that), this should work correctly.

Objects as Dictionaries

hasOwnProperty can also be used in those situations where we have been using the in operator to see whether an object has a specific property. There is one more catch, however. We saw in Chapter 3 that some properties, such as toString, are "hidden" and do not show up when going over properties with for/in. It turns out that browsers in the Gecko family (Firefox, most importantly) give every object a hidden property named __proto__, which points to the prototype of that object. hasOwnProperty will return true for this one, even though the program did not explicitly add it. Having access to the prototype of an object can be very convenient, but making it a property like that was not a very good idea. Still, Firefox is a widely used browser, so when you write a program for the Web, you have to be careful with this. There is a method propertyIsEnumerable, which does mostly the same thing as hasOwnProperty, but also returns false for hidden properties. This allows us to filter out strange things like __proto__.

```
var object = {foo: "bar"};
Object.prototype.propertyIsEnumerable.call(object, "foo");
→ true
```

Nice and simple, no? This is one of the not-so-well-designed aspects of JavaScript. Objects play both the role of "values with methods," for which prototypes are great, and "sets of properties," for which prototypes only get in the way.

Writing the previous expression every time you need to check whether a property is present in an object is awkward. We could put it into a function, but an even better approach is to write a constructor and a prototype specifically for situations like this, where we want to approach an object as just a set of properties. Because you can use it to look things up by name, we will call this type Dictionary.

The Dictionary constructor can be called without arguments, in which case it creates an empty dictionary, or with an object that provides the initial content. It exposes four methods: store to add a value under a given key; lookup to retrieve a value; contains to test whether a key is present; and each, a higher-order function, to iterate over the dictionary's contents.

```
function Dictionary(startValues) {
  this.values = startValues || {};
}
Dictionary.prototype.store = function(name, value) {
  this.values[name] = value;
};
Dictionary.prototype.lookup = function(name) {
  return this.values[name];
};
```

```
Dictionary.prototype.contains = function(name) {
 return Object.prototype.propertyIsEnumerable.call(this.values, name);
};
Dictionary.prototype.each = function(action) {
  forEachIn(this.values, action);
};
```

Here's a small piece of code to test the new type:

```
var colors = new Dictionary({Grover: "blue",
                             Elmo: "red",
                             Bert: "yellow"});
colors.contains("Grover");
→ true
colors.contains("constructor");
→ false

colors.store("Ernie", "orange");
colors.each(function(name, color) {
  print(name, " is ", color);
});
```

Now the whole mess related to approaching objects as plain sets of properties has been "encapsulated" in a convenient interface: one constructor and four methods. Note that the values property of a Dictionary object is not part of this interface; it is an internal detail, and when you are using Dictionary objects, you do not need to directly use it.

Specifying an Interface

Whenever you write an interface, it is a good idea to add a comment with a quick sketch of what it does and how it should be used. This way, when someone, possibly yourself three months after you wrote it, wants to work with the interface, they can quickly see how to use it and do not have to study the whole program.

Most of the time, when you are designing an interface, you will soon find some limitations and problems in whatever you came up with and change it. To prevent wasting your time, it is advisable to document your interfaces only *after* they have been used in a few real situations and proven themselves to be practical. Of course, this might make it tempting to forget about documentation altogether. Personally, I treat writing documentation as a "finishing touch" to add to a system. When it feels ready, it is time to write something about it and to see whether it sounds as good in English (or whatever language) as it does in JavaScript (or whatever programming language).

The distinction between the external interface of an object and its internal details is important for two reasons. First, having a small, clearly described interface makes an object easier to use. You only have to keep the interface in mind, and you do not have to worry about the rest unless you are changing the object itself.

Second, it often turns out to be necessary or practical to change something about the internal implementation of an object type (usually called a *class* in other programming languages) to make it more efficient, for example, or to fix a mistake. When outside code is accessing every single property and detail in the object, you cannot change any of them without also updating a lot of other code. If outside code uses only a small interface, you can do what you want, as long as you do not change the interface.

Some people go very far with this. They will, for example, never include properties in the interface of an object, only methods—if their object type has a length, it will be accessible with the getLength method, not the length property. This way, if they ever want to change their object in such a way that it no longer has a length property, for example because it now has some internal array whose length it must return, they can update the function without changing the interface.

My own take is that in most cases this is not worth it. Adding a getLength method that contains only return this.length; mostly just adds meaningless code, and, in most situations, I consider meaningless code a bigger problem than the risk of having to occasionally change the interface to my objects.

Building an Ecosystem Simulation

In this chapter, we are going to build a virtual terrarium, a tank with insects moving around in it. We will build objects that model the terrarium and the creatures inside it, and we will write methods for those objects to "animate" the creatures and allow them (turn by turn) to live their lives.

Defining the Terrarium

We take a rather simple approach and make the terrarium a two-dimensional grid. On this grid there are a number of bugs. When the terrarium is activated, all the bugs get a chance to take an action, such as moving, which changes the state of the terrarium.

Thus, we chop both time and space into units with a fixed size—squares for space; "turns" for time. This usually makes things easier to model in a program. Of course, it has the drawback of being inaccurate. Fortunately, this terrarium-simulator is not required to be accurate in any way, and we can safely cut corners.

A terrarium can be defined with a "plan," which is an array of strings. We could have used a single string, but the array structure nicely reflects the two-dimensional structure of the data.

```
var thePlan =
  ["############################",
   "#      #    #      o     ##",
   "#                       #",
   "#         #####         #",
   "##        #   #    ##    #",
   "###           ##    #    #",
   "#          ###      #    #",
   "#    ####               #",
   "#    ##       o         #",
   "# o  #         o    ### #",
   "#    #                  #",
   "############################"];
```

The # characters are used to represent the walls of the terrarium (and the ornamental rocks lying in it), the o characters represent bugs, and the spaces are, as you might have guessed, empty space.

Such a plan array can be used to create a terrarium object. This object keeps track of the shape and content of the terrarium and lets the bugs inside move. It has two methods: toString, which converts the terrarium back to a string similar to the plan it was based on so that you can see what is going on inside it, and step, which allows all the bugs in the terrarium to move one step, if they so desire.

Points in Space

The points on the grid will be represented by very simple objects, based on a constructor named Point, which takes two arguments, the x- and y-coordinates of the point, and produces an object with x and y properties. The prototype of this constructor has a single method called add, which takes another point as an argument and returns a *new* point whose x and y are the sum of the x and y of the two given points.

```
function Point(x, y) {
  this.x = x;
  this.y = y;
}
Point.prototype.add = function(other) {
  return new Point(this.x + other.x, this.y + other.y);
};
```

Apart from the constructor and the method, the x and y properties are also part of the interface of this type of objects: Code that uses point objects may freely retrieve and modify x and y.

Representing the Grid

When writing objects to implement a certain program, it is not always very clear which functionality goes where. Some things are best written as methods of your objects, other things are better expressed as separate functions, and some things are best implemented by adding a new type of object. To keep things clear and organized, it is important to keep the amount of methods and responsibilities that an object type has as small as possible. When an object does too much, it becomes a mess and a source of confusion.

I said earlier that the terrarium object will be responsible for storing its contents and for letting the bugs inside it move. Note that it *lets* them move; it doesn't *make* them move. The bugs themselves will also be objects, and these objects are responsible for deciding what they want to do. The terrarium merely provides the infrastructure that asks them what to do, and if they decide to move, it makes sure this happens.

Storing the grid on which the content of the terrarium is kept can get quite complex. It has to define some kind of representation, ways to access this representation, a way to initialize the grid from a "plan" array, a way to write the content of the grid to a string for the toString method, and the movement of the bugs on the grid. It would be nice if part of this could be moved into another object so that the terrarium object itself doesn't get too big and complex.

Whenever you find yourself about to mix data representation and problem-specific code in one data type, don't. Things will be much clearer when the two are kept separate. In this case, we need to represent a grid of values, so I wrote a Grid type, which supports the operations that the terrarium will need.

To store the values on the grid, there are two options. One can use an array of row arrays and use two lookups to get to a specific point, like this:

```
var grid = [["0,0", "1,0", "2,0"],
            ["0,1", "1,1", "2,1"]];
grid[1][2];
→ "2,1"
```

Or, the values can all be put into a single array. In this case, the element at x,y can be found by getting the element at position $x + y * width$ in the array, where width is the width of the grid.

```
var grid = ["0,0", "1,0", "2,0",
            "0,1", "1,1", "2,1"];
grid[2 + 1 * 3];
→ "2,1"
```

I chose the second representation, because it makes it much easier to initialize the array. new Array(x) produces a new array of length x, filled with undefined values.

This code defines the Grid object, with some basic methods:

```
function Grid(width, height) {
  this.width = width;
  this.height = height;
  this.cells = new Array(width * height);
}
Grid.prototype.valueAt = function(point) {
  return this.cells[point.y * this.width + point.x];
};
Grid.prototype.setValueAt = function(point, value) {
  this.cells[point.y * this.width + point.x] = value;
};
Grid.prototype.isInside = function(point) {
  return point.x >= 0 && point.y >= 0 &&
         point.x < this.width && point.y < this.height;
};
Grid.prototype.moveValue = function(from, to) {
  this.setValueAt(to, this.valueAt(from));
  this.setValueAt(from, undefined);
};
```

We will also need to go over all the elements of the grid to find the bugs we need to move or to convert the whole thing to a string. To make this easy, we can use a higher-order function that takes an action as its argument. We add the method each to the prototype of Grid, which takes an action function of two arguments. It calls this function for every point on the grid, giving it the point object for that point as its first argument and giving it the value that is on the grid at that point as its second argument.

This higher-order function abstracts a two-dimensional loop into a single method call:

```
Grid.prototype.each = function(action) {
  for (var y = 0; y < this.height; y++) {
    for (var x = 0; x < this.width; x++) {
      var point = new Point(x, y);
      action(point, this.valueAt(point));
    }
  }
};
```

The double for loop traverses the grid row by row, starting from the top, and then square by square in each row, starting from the left. Doing it in this order is useful, because it will make it easier to write a method that converts the grid to a string—the elements have to appear in the same order in such a string.

A Bug's Programming Interface

Before we can start to write a Terrarium constructor, we will have to get a bit more specific about these "bug objects" that will be living inside it. Earlier, I mentioned that the terrarium will ask the bugs what action they want to take. This will work as follows: Each bug object has an act method that, when called, returns an *action*. An action is an object with a type property, which names the type of action the bug wants to take, for example "move". For most actions, the action also contains extra information, such as the direction the bug wants to go.

Bugs are terribly myopic, and thus they can only see the squares directly around them on the grid. But these they can use to base their action on. When the act method is called, it is given an object with information about the surroundings of the bug in question. For each of the eight directions, it contains a property. The property indicating what is above the bug is called n for north, the one indicating what is above and to the right is called ne for northeast, and so on. To look up the direction these names refer to, the following dictionary object is useful:

```
var directions = new Dictionary(
  {"n":  new Point( 0, -1),
   "ne": new Point( 1, -1),
   "e":  new Point( 1,  0),
   "se": new Point( 1,  1),
   "s":  new Point( 0,  1),
   "sw": new Point(-1,  1),
   "w":  new Point(-1,  0),
   "nw": new Point(-1, -1)});
```

When a bug decides to move, it indicates in which direction it wants to go by giving the resulting action object a direction property that names one of these directions. We can make a simple, stupid bug that always just goes south, "toward the light," like this:

```
function StupidBug() {};
StupidBug.prototype.act = function(surroundings) {
  return {type: "move", direction: "s"};
};
```

The Terrarium Object

Now we can start on the Terrarium object type. Here's its constructor, which takes a plan (an array of strings) as an argument and initializes its grid:

```
var wall = {};

function elementFromCharacter(character) {
```

```
  if (character == " ")
    return undefined;
  else if (character == "#")
    return wall;
  else if (character == "o")
    return new StupidBug();
}

function Terrarium(plan) {
  var grid = new Grid(plan[0].length, plan.length);
  for (var y = 0; y < plan.length; y++) {
    var line = plan[y];
    for (var x = 0; x < line.length; x++) {
      grid.setValueAt(new Point(x, y), elementFromCharacter(line.charAt(x)));
    }
  }
  this.grid = grid;
}
```

The wall variable holds an object that is used to mark the location of walls on the grid. Like a real wall, it doesn't do much; it just sits there and takes up space. The elementFromCharacter function converts a character that is read from the plan into an actual value to store in the grid.

The most straightforward method of a terrarium object is toString, which transforms a terrarium into a string. To make this easier, we mark both the wall and the prototype of the StupidBug with a property character, which holds the character that represents them.

```
wall.character = "#";
StupidBug.prototype.character = "o";

function characterFromElement(element) {
  if (element == undefined)
    return " ";
  else
    return element.character;
}
```

Now we can use the each method of the Grid object to build up a string. But to make the result readable, it would be nice to have a newline at the end of every row. The x-coordinate of the positions on the grid can be used to determine when the end of a line is reached.

```
Terrarium.prototype.toString = function() {
  var characters = [];
  var endOfLine = this.grid.width - 1;
```

```
  this.grid.each(function(point, value) {
    characters.push(characterFromElement(value));
    if (point.x == endOfLine)
      characters.push("\n");
  });
  return characters.join("");
};
```

When you try this by creating a new terrarium based on the plan shown before and then calling toString on it, you'll get a string very similar to the plan you put in.

this and Its Scope

When writing a method like toString shown earlier, which makes use of locally defined functions, you will likely need to access the this variable from an inner function at some point. This will unfortunately not work. Calling a function always results in a new this being defined inside that function, even when it is not used as a method. Thus, any this variable outside of the function will not be visible.

Sometimes it is straightforward to work around this by storing the information you need in a variable, like endOfLine, which *is* visible in the inner function. If you need access to the whole this object, you can store that in a variable too. The name self (or that) is often used for such a variable.

But such pointless extra variables can look messy. Another good solution is to use a function similar to partial from Chapter 5. Instead of adding arguments to a function, this one adds a this object, using it as the first argument to the function's apply method:

```
function bind(func, object) {
  return function(){
    return func.apply(object, arguments);
  };
}

var x = [];
var pushX = bind(x.push, x);
pushX("A");
pushX("B");
x;
→ ["A", "B"]
```

This way, you can bind an inner function to this, and it will have the same this as the outer function.

In the expression bind(x.push, x), the name x still occurs twice. Some people prefer this, more succinct approach to method binding:

```
function method(object, name) {
  return function() {
    return object[name].apply(object, arguments);
  };
}
var pushX = method(x, "push");
```

Animating Life

We will need bind (or method) when implementing the step method of a terrarium. This method has to go over all the bugs on the grid, ask them for an
action, and execute the given action. You might be tempted to use each on
the grid and just handle the bugs we come across. But if you do this, when
a bug moves south or east, we will come across it again in the same turn and
allow it to move again.

Instead, we first gather all the bugs into an array and then process them.
This method gathers bugs, or other things that have an act method, and
stores them in objects that also contain their current position:

```
Terrarium.prototype.listActingCreatures = function() {
  var found = [];
  this.grid.each(function(point, value) {
    if (value != undefined && value.act)
      found.push({object: value, point: point});
  });
  return found;
};
```

When asking a bug to act, we must pass it an object with information
about its current surroundings. This object will use the direction names we
saw earlier ("n", "ne", and so on) as property names. Each property holds a
string of one character, as returned by characterFromElement, indicating what
the bug can see in that direction.

For this, we'll write a method listSurroundings and add it to the Terrarium
prototype. It takes one argument, the point at which the bug is currently
standing, and returns an object with information about the surroundings
of that point. When the point is at the edge of the grid, # is shown for the
directions that would bring the bug outside of the grid, so the bug will not
try to move there.

To go over all the possible directions, we'll just use the each method of
the directions dictionary that we defined before. This will give us the "direction point" objects for those directions (things like Point(0, 1)), which we
can add to the center we were passed in order to get the coordinates we are
interested in.

```
Terrarium.prototype.listSurroundings = function(center) {
  var result = {};
  var grid = this.grid;
  directions.each(function(name, direction) {
    var place = center.add(direction);
    if (grid.isInside(place))
      result[name] = characterFromElement(grid.valueAt(place));
    else
      result[name] = "#";
  });
  return result;
};
```

The two methods defined previously are not part of the external interface of a Terrarium object; they are internal details. Some languages provide ways to explicitly declare certain methods and properties "private" and signal an error when you try to use them from outside the object. JavaScript does not, so you will have to rely on comments to describe the interface to an object. Sometimes it can be useful to use some kind of naming scheme to distinguish between external and internal properties, for example by prefixing all internal ones with an underscore (_). This will make accidental uses of properties that are not part of an object's interface easier to spot.

Next is one more internal helper method, the one that will ask a bug for an action and carry it out. It takes a creature and the point at which the creature is sitting as arguments. For now, it only knows about the "move" action:

```
Terrarium.prototype.processCreature = function(creature) {
  var action = creature.object.act(this.listSurroundings(creature.point));
  if (action.type == "move" && directions.contains(action.direction)) {
    var to = point.add(directions.lookup(action.direction));
    if (this.grid.isInside(to) && this.grid.valueAt(to) == undefined)
      this.grid.moveValue(creature.point, to);
  }
  else {
    throw new Error("Unsupported action: " + action.type);
  }
};
```

Note that it checks whether the chosen direction is inside the grid and empty and ignores it otherwise. This way, the bugs can ask for any action they like—the action will be carried out only if it is actually possible. This acts as a layer of insulation between the bugs and the terrarium and allows us to be less precise when writing the bugs' act methods—for example, the StupidBug just always tries to move south, regardless of any walls that might stand in its way.

These three internal methods then finally allow us to write the step method, which gives all bugs a chance to do something (all elements with an act method—we could also give the wall object one if we so desired and make the walls walk).

```
Terrarium.prototype.step = function() {
  forEach(this.listActingCreatures(), bind(this.processCreature, this));
};
```

It Moves

Let us make a terrarium and see whether anything happens:

```
var terrarium = new Terrarium(thePlan);
terrarium.step();
print(terrarium);
```

If you look closely, you'll notice all the circles are one line below where they started. Here's a before/after view:

```
############################  ############################
#       #   #       o    ## #     #    #            ##
#                     # #                     o      #
#          #####      # #          #####             #
##         #   #   ##  # ##        #   #   ##        #
###          ##   #    # ###          ##   #         #
#          ###    #    # #          ###    #         #
#    ####              # #   ####                    #
#   ##      o          # #   ##                      #
# o  #        o     ### # #     #       o      ### #
#    #                 # # o  #            o         #
############################  ############################
```

Wait, how come the previous calls print(terrarium) and ends up displaying the output of our toString method? print turns its arguments to strings using the String function. Objects are turned to strings by calling their toString method, so giving your own object types a meaningful toString is a good way to make them readable when printed out.

```
Point.prototype.toString = function() {
  return "(" + this.x + "," + this.y + ")";
};
```

More Life Forms

So, we have a terrarium object in which something is happening. But who wants a terrarium with just one kind of bug, and a stupid bug at that? It would be nice if we could add different kinds of bugs. Fortunately, all we have to do is make the elementFromCharacter function more general. Right now, it contains three cases that are typed in directly, or *hard-coded*:

```
function elementFromCharacter(character) {
  if (character == " ")
    return undefined;
  else if (character == "#")
    return wall;
  else if (character == "o")
    return new StupidBug();
}
```

The first two cases we can leave intact, but the last one is way too specific. A better approach would be to store the characters and the corresponding bug constructors in a dictionary and look for them there:

```
var creatureTypes = new Dictionary();
creatureTypes.register = function(constructor, character) {
  constructor.prototype.character = character;
  this.store(character, constructor);
};

function elementFromCharacter(character) {
  if (character == " ")
    return undefined;
  else if (character == "#")
    return wall;
  else if (creatureTypes.contains(character))
    return new (creatureTypes.lookup(character))();
  else
    throw new Error("Unknown character: " + character);
}
```

Note how the register method, which registers a character type, is added to creatureTypes—this is a dictionary object, but there is no reason why it shouldn't support an additional method. This method stores the constructor in the dictionary and makes sure its prototype.character points back at the character so that we can print it.

elementFromCharacter now looks up the character it's given in creatureTypes and raises an exception when it comes across an unknown character.

Here is a new bug type and the call to register its character in creatureTypes:

```
function BouncingBug() {
  this.direction = "ne";
}
BouncingBug.prototype.act = function(surroundings) {
  if (surroundings[this.direction] != " ")
    this.direction = (this.direction == "ne" ? "sw" : "ne");
  return {type: "move", direction: this.direction};
};
creatureTypes.register(BouncingBug, "%");
```

Can you figure out what it does?

The act method checks whether the space ahead (where "ahead" is determined by this.direction) is empty. If it is not, the bug turns around, moving diagonally in the other direction until it hits an obstacle there.

Next up is a bug type called DrunkBug that tries to move in a random direction every turn, never mind whether there is a wall there.

To produce "randomness," we can use the function Math.random. Computers are deterministic machines: They always react in the same way to the input they receive. Thus, they cannot produce truly random values. However, utilities like Math.random are able to produce a series of numbers that look random, even though they are in fact the result of some complicated deterministic computation. The function returns a number between 0 and 1 (0 inclusive, 1 exclusive). To get a whole number instead, we can use a function like this:

```
function randomInteger(below) {
  return Math.floor(Math.random() * below);
}
```

Calling randomInteger(2) will return 0 or 1. The multiplication "scales" up the range of the random number, and calling Math.floor makes sure it becomes a whole number.

To pick a random direction, we will need an array of direction names. We could of course just type ["n", "ne", ...], but that duplicates information, and duplicated information makes us nervous. We could also use the each method in directions to build the array, which is better already.

But there is clearly a generality to be discovered here. Getting a list of the property names in a dictionary sounds like a useful tool to have, so we add it to the Dictionary prototype.

```
Dictionary.prototype.names = function() {
  var names = [];
  this.each(function(name, value) {names.push(name);});
  return names;
};
```

```
directions.names();
→ ["n", "ne", "e", "se", "s", "sw", "w", "nw"]
```

Here, then, is a way to take a random element from an array:

```
function randomElement(array) {
  if (array.length == 0)
    throw new Error("The array is empty.");
  return array[Math.floor(Math.random() * array.length)];
}
```

```
randomElement(["heads", "tails"]);
→ ???
```

The result is shown as ???, because we cannot be sure in advance what the result of that expression will be. In 50% of the cases, it will be "heads"; in the other 50%, it will be "tails".

And here's the bug itself:

```
function DrunkBug() {};
DrunkBug.prototype.act = function(surroundings) {
  return {type: "move", direction: randomElement(directions.names())};
};
creatureTypes.register(DrunkBug, "~");
```

You can test this by adding some % and ~ characters to the plan array, and running a terrarium for a few steps. Notice the bouncing bugs bouncing off the drunk ones? Pure drama.

Polymorphism

We now have several kinds of objects that have an act method and a character property. Because they share these traits, the terrarium can treat them the same way. Thus, we can have all kinds of bugs, without changing anything about the terrarium code. This technique is called *polymorphism*, and it is arguably the most powerful aspect of object-oriented programming.

The basic idea of polymorphism is that when a piece of code is written to work with objects that have a certain interface, any kind of object that happens to support this interface can be plugged into the code, and it will just work. We already saw simple examples of this, like the toString method on objects. All objects that have a meaningful toString method can be given to print, as well as other functions that need to convert values to strings, since they all provide the agreed-on method for that purpose.

Similarly, forEach works on both real arrays and the pseudo-arrays found in the arguments variable, because all it needs is a length property and properties called 0, 1, and so on, for the elements of the array.

A More Lifelike Simulation

To make life in the terrarium more interesting, we will add to it the concepts of food and reproduction. Each living thing in the terrarium gets a new property, energy, which is reduced by performing actions and increased by eating things. When it has enough energy, a thing can reproduce, generating a new creature of the same kind. To keep things reasonably simple, the creatures in our terrarium reproduce asexually, all by themselves.

If there are only bugs, wasting energy by moving around and eating each other, a terrarium will soon succumb to the forces of entropy, run out of energy, and become a lifeless wasteland. To prevent this from happening (too quickly, at least), we add lichen to the terrarium. Lichen do not move; they just use photosynthesis to gather energy and reproduce.

To make this work, we'll need a terrarium with a different processCreature method. We could just replace the method of the Terrarium prototype, but we have become very attached to the simulation of the bouncing and drunk bugs, and we would hate to break our old terrarium.

A solution is to create a new constructor, LifeLikeTerrarium, whose prototype is based on the Terrarium prototype but which has a different processCreature method.

Inheritance

There are a few ways to do this. We could go over the properties of Terrarium.prototype and add them one by one to LifeLikeTerrarium.prototype. This is easy to do, and in some cases it is the best solution, but in this case there is a cleaner way. If we make the old prototype object the prototype of the new prototype object (you may have to reread that a few times), it will automatically have all its properties.

Unfortunately, JavaScript does not have a straightforward way to create an object whose prototype is a certain other object. It is possible to write a function that does this, though, by using the following trick:

```
function clone(object) {
  function OneShotConstructor(){}
  OneShotConstructor.prototype = object;
  return new OneShotConstructor();
}
```

This function uses an empty one-shot constructor, whose prototype is the given object. When using new on this constructor, it will create a new object based on the argument object.

```
function LifeLikeTerrarium(plan) {
  Terrarium.call(this, plan);
}
LifeLikeTerrarium.prototype = clone(Terrarium.prototype);
LifeLikeTerrarium.prototype.constructor = LifeLikeTerrarium;
```

The new constructor doesn't need to do anything different from the old one, so it just calls the old one on the this object. We also have to restore the constructor property in the new prototype, or it would claim its constructor is Terrarium (which, of course, is relevant only if we were to make use of this property, which we don't).

It is now possible to replace some of the methods of the LifeLikeTerrarium object or add new ones. We have based a new object type on an old one, which saved us the work of rewriting all the methods that are the same in Terrarium and LifeLikeTerrarium. This technique is called *inheritance*. The new type inherits the properties of the old type. In most cases, this means the new type will still support the interface of the old type, though it might also support a few methods that the old type does not have. This way, objects of the new type can be (polymorphically) used in all the places where objects of the old type could be used.

In most programming languages with explicit support for object-oriented programming, inheritance is a very straightforward thing. In Java-Script, the language doesn't really specify a simple way to do it. Because of this, JavaScript programmers have invented many different approaches to inheritance, but none of them is quite perfect. Fortunately, such a broad range of approaches allows a programmer to choose the most suitable one for the problem at hand and allows certain tricks that would be utterly impossible in other languages.

At the end of this chapter, we will see a few other ways to implement inheritance and the issues they have.

Keeping Track of Energy

The new processCreature method is a lot more complicated than the old one—instead of one type of action, it supports five different types. It uses some helper methods so that it doesn't become a huge monster of a method:

```
LifeLikeTerrarium.prototype.processCreature = function(creature) {
  var energy, action, self = this;
  function dir() {
    if (!directions.contains(action.direction)) return null;
    var target = point.add(directions.lookup(action.direction));
    if (!self.grid.isInside(target)) return null;
    return target;
  }

action = creature.object.act(this.listSurroundings(creature.point));

  if (action.type == "move")
    energy = this.creatureMove(creature.object, creature.point, dir());
  else if (action.type == "eat")
    energy = this.creatureEat(creature.object, dir());
  else if (action.type == "photosynthesize")
    energy = -1;
```

```
else if (action.type == "reproduce")
  energy = this.creatureReproduce(creature.object, dir());
else if (action.type == "wait")
  energy = 0.2;
else
  throw new Error("Unsupported action: " + action.type);

creature.object.energy -= energy;
if (creature.object.energy <= 0)
  this.grid.setValueAt(creature.point, undefined);
};
```

The local `dir` function (using the `self` variable to access `this`) is used to extract a direction from an action, doing some error checking on it. If it finds something invalid, it returns `null`. The helper functions will be written to check their argument so that actions with invalid directions are simply ignored.

Each helper returns the amount of energy spent by this action or a negative number when energy is gained. The code at the end of the function updates the creature's energy score and removes the creature from the grid when it runs out of energy.

The action-specific helpers are relatively straightforward:

```
LifeLikeTerrarium.prototype.creatureMove = function(creature, from, to) {
  if (to != null && this.grid.valueAt(to) == undefined) {
    this.grid.moveValue(from, to);
    from.x = to.x; from.y = to.y;
  }
  return 1;
};
```

As before, this checks whether the chosen direction is valid, and not obstructed, and then moves. The one awkward part is that this has to update the `from` object, because otherwise the code in `processCreature` that removes dead creatures won't know where to find this creature anymore.

Eating is not hard either. It locates the meal that the creature has chosen, checks whether there is actually anything there, and checks whether this anything has energy (so that creatures don't go around eating walls), and then it removes the meal from the grid, giving its energy to the creature.

```
LifeLikeTerrarium.prototype.creatureEat = function(creature, source) {
  var energy = 1;
  if (source != null) {
    var meal = this.grid.valueAt(source);
    if (meal != undefined && meal.energy) {
      this.grid.setValueAt(source, undefined);
      energy -= meal.energy;
    }
}
```

```
  }
  return energy;
};
```

Finally, to reproduce, we again check whether the chosen spot is valid and empty (a creature has to choose a spot to put its child). If it is, a new creature of the same type as the parent is created. The amount of energy the parent will lose for reproducing is twice the amount of energy the new creature gets (childbearing is not easy). If the parent does not have that much energy, the child is not put onto the grid.

```
LifeLikeTerrarium.prototype.creatureReproduce = function(creature, target) {
  var energy = 1;
  if (target != null && this.grid.valueAt(target) == undefined) {
    var species = characterFromElement(creature);
    var baby = elementFromCharacter(species);
    energy = baby.energy * 2;
    if (creature.energy >= energy)
      this.grid.setValueAt(target, baby);
  }
  return energy;
};
```

Adding Plant Life

We now have the "framework" needed to simulate these more lifelike creatures. We could put the creatures from the old terrarium into it, but they would just die after a few turns. So, let's make some new ones. First we'll make the lichen, which are rather simple. We will use the character * to represent them.

This again uses the randomElement function introduced when we wrote the drunk bug. It also defines a findDirections function, which is used to enumerate the directions in which a certain type of character is being seen by the creature.

```
function findDirections(surroundings, wanted) {
  var found = [];
  directions.each(function(name) {
    if (surroundings[name] == wanted)
      found.push(name);
  });
  return found;
}

function Lichen() {
  this.energy = 5;
}
```

```
Lichen.prototype.act = function(surroundings) {
  var emptySpace = findDirections(surroundings, " ");
  if (this.energy >= 13 && emptySpace.length > 0)
    return {type: "reproduce", direction: randomElement(emptySpace)};
  else if (this.energy < 20)
    return {type: "photosynthesize"};
  else
    return {type: "wait"};
};
creatureTypes.register(Lichen, "*");
```

Lichen do not grow bigger than 20 energy, or they would get *huge* when they are surrounded by other lichen and have no room to reproduce.

The Herbivore

Next up is the `LichenEater`. It starts with an energy of 10, and its behavior can be described like this:

- When it has an energy of 30 or more and there is room near it, it reproduces.

- Otherwise, if there are lichen nearby, it eats a random one.

- Otherwise, if there is space to move, it moves into a random nearby empty square.

- Otherwise, it waits.

We'll use the `c` character (Pac-Man) for this creature:

```
function LichenEater() {
  this.energy = 10;
}
LichenEater.prototype.act = function(surroundings) {
  var emptySpace = findDirections(surroundings, " ");
  var lichen = findDirections(surroundings, "*");

  if (this.energy >= 30 && emptySpace.length > 0)
    return {type: "reproduce", direction: randomElement(emptySpace)};
  else if (lichen.length > 0)
    return {type: "eat", direction: randomElement(lichen)};
  else if (emptySpace.length > 0)
    return {type: "move", direction: randomElement(emptySpace)};
  else
    return {type: "wait"};
};
creatureTypes.register(LichenEater, "c");
```

Bringing It to Life

And that gives us enough elements to try our new terrarium. Imagine a moody, dark cave, with lichen growing on the walls and lichen-eating bugs scuttling around on the floor. That's what this code is trying to express:

```
var moodyCave =
  ["#############################",
   "#                     #####",
   "#   ***              **##",
   "#   *##**        ** c  *##",
   "#   ***    c    ##**    *#",
   "#       c       ##***   *#",
   "#               ##**    *#",
   "#   c     #*            *#",
   "#*        #**       c   *#",
   "#***      ##**    c    **#",
   "#*****    ###***       *###",
   "#############################"];

var terrarium = new LifeLikeTerrarium(moodyCave);
for (var i = 0; i < 10; i++) {
  for (var j = 0; j < 20; j++)
    terrarium.step();
  print(terrarium);
}
```

The following output shows a typical run of such a terrarium, with steps of 20 turns between the pictures:

```
#############################  #############################
#   ******        c    ######  # c  c*****          ######
#   ******    c    c  ***##    #    c*****          ****##
#   **##***        c      ***##   # c ##***          ****##
#     ** *         ##     ***#  # c  * *          ##  c ***#
# cc ***           ##c    ***#  #    c      c   ##  cc***#
#          c      ## c   ***#   #    c      c   ##   ****#
# c         # **c        ***#   # c  c      #  c  *******#
#           #****c    * ***# #*    c c      #   *  *******#
#******     ##*****      ****# #*c  c   c  ## c  * *******#
#******     ###*****     **### #**   cc     ###   c   ****###
#############################  #############################
```

```
############################# #############################
#  c cc   **        c###### #        ***       ######
#        c *        c  ## #        ****          ##
#   ##    *         c## #  ##    **              ##
#   cc   *       ##ccc    # #          *    ##     #
#c              ## c  cc# #      c        ##    c #
#    c      c c##   ccc # #               ##      #
#         #     cc cc  # #          #            #
#         #       c  c# #          c#        c  #
#        ##    c  c  c  # #        ##            #
#       ###      c  c ### #       ###      c  ###
############################# #############################


############################# #############################
#         **        ###### #                    ######
#         **          ## #                        ##
#   ##    **          ## #  ##                    ##
#        *      ##       # #              ##      #
#        c      ##    c # #               ##      #
#               ##       # #              ##      #
#        #            # #        #              #
#        c#        c  # #        #              #
#        ##          # #        ##              #
#       ###      c  ### #       ###          ###
############################# #############################
```

Most of the time, the lichen quickly overgrow a large part of the terrarium, after which the abundance of food makes the eaters so numerous that they wipe out all (or nearly all) the lichen and thus themselves. Ah, tragedies of nature.

Artificial Stupidity

Having the inhabitants of our terrarium go extinct after a few minutes is kind of depressing. To deal with this, we could teach our lichen-eaters about long-term sustainable farming. By making them eat only if they see at least two lichen nearby, no matter how hungry they are, they will never exterminate the lichen. This can be done by changing their act method to eat only when lichen.length is at least 2.

Running the previous moodyCave terrarium with this change, we still usually see the lichen-eaters still go extinct after a while, because, in a time of starvation, they crawl aimlessly back and forth through empty space, instead of finding the lichen that is sitting just a few squares away from them.

Another potential improvement is to reduce the randomness of these creatures' movement. By always picking a random direction, it will often move back and forth without getting anywhere. By remembering the last direction it went, and preferring that direction, the eater will waste less time and find food faster. Here is the updated implementation:

```
function CleverLichenEater() {
  this.energy = 10;
  this.direction = "ne";
}
CleverLichenEater.prototype.act = function(surroundings) {
  var emptySpace = findDirections(surroundings, " ");
  var lichen = findDirections(surroundings, "*");

  if (surroundings[this.direction] != " " && emptySpace.length > 0)
    this.direction = randomElement(emptySpace);

  if (this.energy >= 30 && emptySpace.length > 0)
    return {type: "reproduce", direction: randomElement(emptySpace)};
  else if (lichen.length > 1)
    return {type: "eat", direction: randomElement(lichen)};
  else if (emptySpace.length > 0)
    return {type: "move", direction: this.direction};
  else
    return {type: "wait"};
};
creatureTypes.register(CleverLichenEater, "c");
```

When used in the simulation, this new animal survives the moody cave a bit longer than its simple-minded cousin. If you give it a big enough world to live in, so that abundance and scarcity occur in parts of the environment, rather than everywhere at once, the ecosystem even seems to stay stable.

Prototypal Inheritance

The whole terrarium detour should have given you some insight into the way objects are used in real programs. The rest of the chapter is devoted to a more in-depth look at inheritance and the problems related to inheritance in JavaScript.

First, let's go over some theory. Students of object-oriented programming can often be heard having lengthy, subtle discussions about correct and incorrect uses of inheritance. It is important to bear in mind that inheritance, in the end, is just a trick that allows lazy programmers—and here I mean to use the word *lazy* in the most positive way possible—to write less code. Thus, the question of whether inheritance is being used correctly boils down to the question of whether the resulting code works properly and avoids useless repetition. Still, the principles used by these students provide a good way to start thinking about inheritance.

Inheritance is the creation of a new type of objects, the *subtype*, based on an existing type, the *supertype*. The subtype starts with all the properties and methods of the supertype (it inherits them) and then modifies a few of these or adds new ones. Inheritance is best used when the thing modeled by the subtype can be said to *be* an object of the supertype.

Thus, a `Piano` type could be a subtype of an `Instrument` type, because a piano *is* an instrument. Since a piano has a whole array of keys, one might be tempted to make `Piano` a subtype of `Array`, but a piano *is* no array, and implementing it like that is bound to lead to all kinds of silliness. For example, a piano also has pedals. Why would `piano[0]` give me the first key, and not the first pedal? The situation is, in fact, that a piano *has* keys, so it would be better to give it a property `keys` and possibly another property `pedals`, both holding arrays.

It is possible for a subtype to be the supertype of yet another subtype. Some problems are best solved by building a complex family tree of types. You have to take care not to get too inheritance-happy, though. Inheritance has its own way of tangling code together, and overusing it usually produces a tightly connected mess that can be hard to modify.

Type-Definition Utilities

The workings of the `new` keyword and the `prototype` property of constructors suggest a certain way of defining types, which we've been using so far. For simple objects, such as the terrarium creatures, this way works rather well. Unfortunately, when a program starts to make serious use of inheritance, this approach to objects quickly becomes clumsy. Adding some functions to take care of common operations can make things a little smoother. Many people define, for example, `inherit` and `method` methods on objects.

```
Object.prototype.inherit = function(baseConstructor) {
  this.prototype = clone(baseConstructor.prototype);
  this.prototype.constructor = this;
};
Object.prototype.method = function(name, func) {
  this.prototype[name] = func;
};
```

Having these, we can write code like this:

```
function StrangeArray(){}
StrangeArray.inherit(Array);
StrangeArray.method("push", function(value) {
  Array.prototype.push.call(this, value);
  Array.prototype.push.call(this, value);
});
```

```
var strange = new StrangeArray();
strange.push(4);
→ [4, 4]
```

If you search the Web for the words *JavaScript* and *inheritance*, you will come across scores of different variations on this, some of them quite a lot more complex and clever than this code.

Note how the push method written here uses the push method from the prototype of its parent type. This is something that is done often when using inheritance—a method in the subtype internally uses a method of the supertype but extends it somehow.

Prototypes as Types

The biggest problem with this basic approach is the duality between constructors and prototypes. Constructors take a very central role; they are the things that give an object type its name, and when you need to get at a prototype, you have to go to the constructor and take its prototype property.

Not only does this lead to a *lot* of typing ("prototype" is nine letters, after all), it is also confusing. We had to write an empty, useless constructor for StrangeArray in the previous example. Quite a few times, I have found myself accidentally adding methods to a constructor instead of its prototype or trying to call Array.slice when I really meant Array.prototype.slice. In a way, the prototype itself is the most important aspect of an object type, and the constructor is just an extension of that, a special kind of method.

With a few simple helper methods added to Object.prototype, it is possible to create an alternative approach to objects and inheritance. In this approach, a type is represented by its prototype, and we will use capitalized variables to store these prototypes. When it needs to do any "constructing" work, this is done by a method called construct. We add a method called create to the Object prototype, which is used in place of the new keyword. It clones the object and calls its construct method, if there is such a method, giving it the arguments that were passed to create.

```
Object.prototype.create = function() {
  var object = clone(this);
  if (object.construct != undefined)
    object.construct.apply(object, arguments);
  return object;
};
```

Inheritance can be done by cloning a prototype object and adding or replacing some of its properties. We also provide a convenient shorthand for this, an extend method, which clones the object it is applied to and adds to this clone the properties in the object that it is given as an argument.

```
Object.prototype.extend = function(properties) {
  var result = clone(this);
```

```
  forEachIn(properties, function(name, value) {
    result[name] = value;
  });
  return result;
};
```

In a situation where it is not safe to mess with the Object prototype, these can, of course, be implemented as regular (nonmethod) functions.

A World of Objects

Here's an example. If you are old enough, you may at one time have played a "text adventure" game, where you move through a virtual world by typing commands and getting textual descriptions of the things around you and the actions you perform. Now those were games!

We could write the prototype for an item in such a game, the things the game world is built out of, like this:

```
var Item = {
  construct: function(name) {
    this.name = name;
  },
  inspect: function() {
    print("it is ", this.name, ".");
  },
  kick: function() {
    print("klunk!");
  },
  take: function() {
    print("you cannot lift ", this.name, ".");
  }
};

var lantern = Item.create("the brass lantern");
lantern.kick();
```

You can then inherit from it like this:

```
var DetailedItem = Item.extend({
  construct: function(name, details) {
    Item.construct.call(this, name);
    this.details = details;
  },
  inspect: function() {
    print("you see ", this.name, ". ", this.details, ".");
  }
});
```

```
var giantSloth =
  DetailedItem.create("the giant sloth",
                      "it is quietly hanging from a tree, munching leaves");
giantSloth.inspect();
```

Leaving out the compulsory prototype part makes tasks such as calling Item.construct from DetailedItem's constructor slightly simpler. Note that it would be a bad idea to just do this.name = name in DetailedItem.construct. This duplicates a line. Sure, duplicating the line is shorter than calling the Item.construct function, but if we end up adding something to this constructor later, we have to add it in two places.

Most of the time, a subtype's constructor should start by calling the constructor of the supertype. This way, it starts with a valid object of the supertype, which it can then extend. In this new approach to prototypes, types that need no constructor can leave it out. They will automatically inherit the constructor of their supertype. This can be seen in the follwing subtype:

```
var SmallItem = Item.extend({
  kick: function() {
    print(this.name, " flies across the room.");
  },
  take: function() {
    // (imagine some code that moves the item to your pocket here)
    print("you take ", this.name, ".");
  }
});

var pencil = SmallItem.create("the red pencil");
pencil.take();
```

Even though SmallItem does not define its own constructor, creating it with a name argument works, because it inherited the constructor from the Item prototype.

The instanceof Operator

JavaScript has an operator called instanceof, which can be used to determine whether an object is based on a certain prototype. You give it the object on the left side and a constructor on the right side, and it returns a Boolean, true if the constructor's prototype property is the direct or indirect prototype of the object and false otherwise. For example, [] instanceof Array will produce true.

When you are not using regular constructors, using this operator becomes rather clumsy—it expects a constructor function as its second argument, but we only have prototypes. A trick similar to the clone function can be used to get around it: We use a "fake constructor" and apply instanceof to it.

```
Object.prototype.isA = function(prototype) {
  function DummyConstructor() {}
  DummyConstructor.prototype = prototype;
  return this instanceof DummyConstructor;
};
```

```
pencil.isA(Item);
```
→ true
```
pencil.isA(DetailedItem);
```
→ false

Mixing Types

Next, we want to make a small item that has a detailed description. It seems like this item would have to inherit both from DetailedItem and from SmallItem. JavaScript does not allow an object to have multiple prototypes, and even if it did, the problem would not be quite that easy to solve. For example, if SmallItem would, for some reason, also define an inspect method, which inspect method should the new prototype use?

Deriving an object type from more than one parent type is called *multiple inheritance*. Some languages chicken out and forbid it altogether; others define complicated schemes to make it work in a well-defined way. It is possible to implement a decent multiple-inheritance framework in JavaScript. In fact, there are multiple good approaches to this—but they all are too complex to be discussed here. Instead, I will show a very simple approach that suffices in most cases.

A *mix-in* is a specific kind of prototype that can be "mixed into" other prototypes. SmallItem can be seen as such a prototype. By copying its kick and take methods into another prototype, we mix smallness into this prototype.

```
function mixInto(object, mixIn) {
  forEachIn(mixIn, function(name, value) {
    object[name] = value;
  });
};
```

```
var SmallDetailedItem = clone(DetailedItem);
mixInto(SmallDetailedItem, SmallItem);
```

```
var deadMouse = SmallDetailedItem.create("Fred the mouse", "he is dead");
deadMouse.inspect();
deadMouse.kick();
```

This will print the following:

```
you see Fred the mouse. he is dead.
Fred the mouse flies across the room.
```

Remember that forEachIn goes over the object's *own* properties only, so it will copy kick and take but not the constructor that SmallItem inherited from Item.

Mixing prototypes gets more complex when the mix-in has a constructor or when some of its methods "clash" with methods in the prototype that it is mixed into. Sometimes, it is workable to do a "manual mix-in." Say we have a prototype Monster, which has its own constructor, and we want to mix that with DetailedItem:

```
var Monster = Item.extend({
  construct: function(name, dangerous) {
    Item.construct.call(this, name);
    this.dangerous = dangerous;
  },
  kick: function() {
    if (this.dangerous)
      print(this.name, " bites your head off.");
    else
      print(this.name, " squeaks and runs away.");
  }
});

var DetailedMonster = DetailedItem.extend({
  construct: function(name, description, dangerous) {
    DetailedItem.construct.call(this, name, description);
    Monster.construct.call(this, name, dangerous);
  },
  kick: Monster.kick
});

var giantSloth = DetailedMonster.create(
  "the giant sloth",
  "it is quietly hanging from a tree, munching leaves",
  true);
giantSloth.kick();
```

But note that this causes Item constructor to be called twice when creating a DetailedMonster—once through the DetailedItem constructor and once through the Monster constructor. In this case, there is not much harm done, but there are situations where this would cause problems.

Don't let those complications discourage you from making use of inheritance. Multiple inheritance, though extremely useful in some situations, can be safely ignored most of the time. This is why languages like Java get away with forbidding it. And if, at some point, you find that you really need multiple inheritance, you can search the Web, do some research, and figure out an approach that works for your situation.

7

MODULARITY

Imagine a program consisting of, say, 100 different functions. By most standards, that's a small program. If we end up changing the list of arguments passed to one of those functions, which other functions do we have to modify? If we change some of the code, how do we find out whether any of the other functions have become obsolete? If we need one of the functions for another program, how many of the other functions also have to be added to that other program, because they are used by the function we need?

If there is no organization at all to your program, finding the answer to any of these questions means going through all of the functions. There are of course tools that can help us here, such as the Unix utility grep, but, especially in the case where you need to reuse some functionality in another project, you are still going to need a lot of manual code shuffling.

To make such interdependence of code easier to keep track of, experienced programmers try to divide their programs into *modules*, each with its own task, and minimize the amount of "coupling" between these modules—the amount of detail the modules have to "know" about each other.

Modules

A module can be any collection of functions and values that, together, fulfill some specialized role. Many languages have a built-in way to define modules, but—once again—JavaScript leaves us in the cold. Like with the object interfaces we saw in Chapter 6, modules have to exist purely in the minds of the programmers (and, ideally, in their comments and documentation).

Object interfaces and modules are in fact related concepts. A module should expose an interface just like an object does. In fact, a module can consist of just a single object (and its interface). The Dictionary object we created in the previous chapter is an example of an object that would make a good module.

A module does not have to stand on its own. Often, when building a module, functionality from other modules is useful. The Dictionary object, for example, uses the forEachIn function, which should probably be part of some utility module. Such dependencies should be noted, so that when you change a module, you know which modules depend on it and should also be updated.

An Example

In Chapter 6, while developing a terrarium, we used a number of functions described in Chapter 5. Chapter 6 also defined a few new concepts that had nothing in particular to do with terraria, such as clone and the Dictionary type. All these things were haphazardly added to the environment. This is one way to split this program into modules:

- A module Utilities, which contains things such as forEach, map, reduce, forEachIn, and clone, and which depends on nothing

- Dictionary, containing the dictionary type and depending on Utilities

- And finally the Terrarium module, which depends on both of the previous modules

A module that *depends* on another module will work only when this other module is also loaded. It is a good idea to try to avoid circles in dependencies (A depending on B, with B depending on A). Not only do circular dependencies create a practical problem (if module A and B depend on each other, which one should be loaded first?), they also make the relation between the modules less straightforward and can result in a tangle of modules that are just as hard to track as a nonmodularized program.

Modules as Files

One obvious way to separate modules is by putting every module in a different file. This makes it clear which code belongs to which module. I should note, though, that when you are building a website and you have a lot of small module files, you should probably combine all those files into a big file before deploying them to the Web, because loading lots of small files tends to make a website slow.

Browsers load JavaScript files when they find a `<script>` tag with an `src` attribute in the HTML of the web page. The extension `.js` is usually used for files containing JavaScript code. For example, you could have a file `map.js`, containing this version of `map`:

```
function map(func, array) {
  var len = array.length, result = new Array(len);
  for (var i = 0; i < len; i++)
    result[i] = func(array[i]);
  return result;
}
```

If you have this file available on your web server under `/js/map.js`, you'd put a line like this into your HTML document to make the function available on the page:

```
<script src="/js/map.js" type="text/javascript"></script>
```

Now any other scripts loaded on the page will be able to use the `map` function. For a proper discussion about the way JavaScript programs are used in web pages, see Chapter 9.

A script tag like this can also be used without the `src` attribute but with a JavaScript program enclosed between the opening and closing tags. Here's an example:

```
<script type="text/javascript">alert("Hi!");</script>
```

The Shape of a Module

Since the language does not prescribe a way to write modules, we will have to come up with some techniques of our own. For modules that consist of only a few functions or objects (or just one), there's not much to think about—you just write those functions or objects as usual and call it a module.

For bigger modules or modules that contain some "internal" elements—variables that are used by the module's code but not part of its interface—there are reasons to do things differently.

In JavaScript, "top-level" variables all live together in a single space. When a lot of code is loaded into an environment, it becomes hard to keep track of which variable names are used, which makes it very easy to accidentally use a name that was already used for something else. This will, of course, break the code that used the original value. The proliferation of top-level variables is called *namespace pollution*, and it can be a rather severe problem in JavaScript. The language will not warn you when you redefine an existing variable; things will just break.

For this reason, bigger modules should try to use as few top-level variable names as possible and not put their internal variables into the top-level environment.

Functions as Local Namespaces

We have a very simple module for translating between month names and their numbers (as used by Date, where January is 0). It uses an internal variable names:

```
var names = ["January", "February", "March", "April", "May", "June", "July",
             "August", "September", "October", "November", "December"];
function getMonthName(number) {return names[number];}
function getMonthNumber(name) {
  for (var number = 0; number < names.length; number++) {
    if (names[number] == name) return number;
  }
}

getMonthNumber("February");
→ 1
```

The standard trick for hiding names from the rest of the world is to use a function as a local module namespace. The whole module is written inside a function, and the interface of the module is explicitly put into the top-level environment. It does that by setting properties in the window object, which is an object whose properties represent the top-level variables. Thus, adding properties to the object causes variables to be defined.

```
function buildMonthNameModule() {
  var names = ["January", "February", "March", "April", "May", "June", "July",
               "August", "September", "October", "November", "December"];
  function getMonthName(number) {return names[number];}
  function getMonthNumber(name) {
    for (var number = 0; number < names.length; number++) {
      if (names[number] == name) return number;
    }
  }

  window.getMonthName = getMonthName;
  window.getMonthNumber = getMonthNumber;
}
buildMonthNameModule();
```

This way, the module's functions and variables can all see each other, but "outsiders" can only see the interface.

We can make this a little more elegant by using a helper function, provide, which can be given an object containing an object that describes the interface, with property names indicating the variable names and with property values indicating the values those variables should get. provide will set these variables in the global scope:

```
function provide(values) {
  forEachIn(values, function(name, value) {
    window[name] = value;
  });
}
```

To shorten the code a little more, we can write the local-scope function as an anonymous function and call it directly:

```
(function() {
  var names = ["January", "February", "March", "April", "May", "June", "July",
               "August", "September", "October", "November", "December"];
  provide({
    getMonthName: function(number) {return names[number];},
    getMonthNumber: function(name) {
      for (var number = 0; number < names.length; number++) {
        if (names[number] == name) return number;
      }
    }
  });
})();
```

I wouldn't recommend writing modules like this right from the start. While you are still working on a piece of code, it is easier to just use the simple approach we have used so far and put everything in the top-level environment. That way, you can inspect the module's internal values in your browser and test them. Once a module is more or less finished, it is not difficult to wrap it in a function.

Module Objects

Some modules export so many variables that it is a bad idea to put them all into the top-level environment. These have to be handled differently. You can do what the standard Math object does and represent the module as a single object whose properties are the functions and values it exports. Here's an example:

```
var HTML = {
  tag: function(name, content, properties) {
    return {name: name, properties: properties, content: content};
  },
```

```
  link: function(target, text) {
    return HTML.tag("a", [text], {href: target});
  }
  /* ... many, many more HTML-producing functions ... */
};
```

Note that such an object is analogous to the "interface objects" we passed to provide earlier. In fact, it *can* also be passed to that function, which will have the effect of "importing" the module into the global namespace. This can occasionally be useful when you are using a module a lot and don't want to retype the object name all the time. (But of course, you have to watch out for name collisions.)

Internal variables in a module object can be made normal properties of the object, or you can use the function trick described earlier and have the scope function return the module object instead of setting global variables:

```
var days = (function() {
  var names = ["Sunday", "Monday", "Tuesday", "Wednesday",
               "Thursday", "Friday", "Saturday"];
  return {
    getDayName: function(number) {return names[number];},
    getDayNumber: function(name) {
      for (var number = 0; number < names.length; number++) {
        if (names[number] == name) return number;
      }
    }
  };
})();

days.getDayNumber("Wednesday");
→ 3
```

Interface Design

Designing an interface for a module or an object type is one of the subtler aspects of programming. Any nontrivial functionality can be exposed in different ways. Finding a way that works well is something of an art.

The best way to learn the value of good interface design is, unfortunately, to use bad interfaces. Once you get fed up with them, you'll figure out a way to improve them and learn a lot in the process. Try not to assume that a lousy interface is "just the way it is." Fix it, or wrap it in a new interface that is better (we will see an example of this in Chapter 10).

Predictability

If programmers can predict the way your interface works, they (or you) won't need to look things up while working. Thus, try to follow conventions (such as using camelCase normal names and Capitalized constructor names) as much as possible. When there is another module or part of the standard JavaScript functionality that does something similar to what you are implementing, it might be a good idea to make your interface resemble the existing interface. That way, people who know the existing interface will feel right at home.

Composability

In your interfaces, try to use the simplest data structures that work and make functions do a single, clear thing—if possible, they should be pure functions (see Chapter 2).

For example, it is not uncommon for modules to provide their own array-like collection objects, with their own interface for extracting elements from such an object, and return those from functions that return collections of things. Such objects cannot be passed to map or forEach. This is a case of bad *composability*, since the module cannot be easily composed with algorithms operating on arrays.

Another example would be a module for spellchecking text, which we might need when we want to write a text editor. The spellchecker could be made to operate directly on whichever complicated data structures the editor uses and directly call internal functions in the editor to have the user choose between spelling suggestions. If we do that, the module cannot be used with any other programs. On the other hand, if we define the spellchecking interface so that you can pass it a simple string and it will return the position in the string where it found a possible misspelling, along with an array of suggested corrections, then we have an interface that could also be composed with other systems.

Layered Interfaces

When designing an interface for a complex piece of functionality (say, sending email), you often run into something of a dilemma. On the one hand, you do not want to overload the user of your interface with details. They shouldn't have to study your interface for 20 minutes before they can send an email. On the other hand, you do not want to hide all the details either—when people need to do complicated things with your module, that should also be possible.

Often the solution is to provide two interfaces: a detailed "low-level" one for advanced use and a simple "high-level" one for straightforward situations. The second one can usually be built very easily using the tools provided by the first one. In the email module, the high-level interface could just be a function that takes a message, a sender address, and a receiver address, and sends the email. The low-level interface allows full control over email headers, attachments, sending HTML mail, and so on.

Argument Objects

There are functions that require a lot of arguments. Sometimes this means they are just badly designed, and the problem can be remedied by splitting them into a few more focused functions. But in other cases, the function really needs all those arguments. Typically, some of the arguments have a sensible default value.

For example, the following function can be used to find the position of a value in an array, with extra optional arguments that allow you to search just part of the array (start and end) and to use a custom function as a replacement for == when comparing elements (compare).

```
function positionOf(element, array, compare, start, end) {
  if (start == null) start = 0;
  if (end == null) end = array.length;
  for (; start < end; start++) {
    var current = array[start];
    if (compare ? compare(element, current) : element == current) return start;
  }
}
```

```
positionOf(2, [1, 2, 3, 4, 3, 2, 1], null, 3, 6);
→ 5
```

Remember that == null returns true both if the value is null and if it is undefined. This is used to check whether start and end were passed and to give them a useful default value if they weren't.

In the example call shown after the function, the disadvantage of having so many optional arguments becomes clear. We have to pass null to "skip" an argument, and when you read the call, you have to actually count along with the arguments to understand which value has which role. We can improve this by wrapping the optional arguments in an object:

```
// optional arguments in args: {compare, start, end}
function positionOf(element, array, args) {
  args = args || {};
  var start = (args.start == null ? 0 : args.start),
      end = (args.end == null) ? array.length : args.end,
      compare = args.compare;
  for (; start < end; start++) {
    var current = array[start];
    if (compare ? compare(element, current) : element == current) return start;
  }
}
```

```
positionOf(2, [1, 2, 3, 4, 3, 2, 1], {start: 3, end: 6});
→ 5
```

The call becomes more readable like this. However, it has become harder to figure out which arguments are supported. This is why I have put the comment before the function, listing the optional arguments.

Libraries

A module or group of modules intended to be used in more than one program is usually called a *library*. For common, well-defined problems, you can usually find libraries online, often released under some license that allows you to use them in your projects for free (make sure you check, though).

Some languages have a well-organized collection of quality libraries, either bundled with the language itself or available in a central place on the Web. JavaScript has no such thing yet, so you will just have to use a search engine to look around. And of course, there is also a lot of junk online, so treat libraries from unknown sources with caution—they might be broken, and they might even contain malicious code.

There are currently a number of different popular libraries providing a "fundamental" set of tools, each with its own focus. These usually contain equivalents of most of the general utilities we use in this book. Once you get serious about JavaScript programming, it pays to read the documentation for a few of the major ones and see which one you like best. (As a starting point, search the Web for jQuery, YUI, Prototype, and ExtJS.)

The fact that a basic toolkit is almost indispensable for any nontrivial JavaScript programs, combined with the fact that there are so many different toolkits, causes a bit of a dilemma for library writers. You either have to make your library depend on one of the toolkits or write the basic tools yourself and include them with the library. The first option makes the library hard to use for people who are using a different toolkit, and the second option adds a lot of nonessential code to the library. This is probably the reason why a lot of libraries can still only be found as, for example, "jQuery plug-ins" or "YUI components," not plain-vanilla JavaScript libraries.

8

REGULAR EXPRESSIONS

At various points in the previous chapters, we had to look for patterns in string values. In Chapter 3 we extracted date values from strings by writing out the precise positions at which the numbers that were part of the date could be found. Later, in Chapter 5, we saw some particularly ugly pieces of code for finding certain types of characters in a string, for example the characters that had to be escaped in HTML output.

Regular expressions are a language for describing patterns in string data. They form a small, separate language, which is embedded inside JavaScript (as well as various other programming languages). This language is very succinct, though not very readable—big regular expressions tend to look like cartoon characters cursing. Regardless, they are a powerful tool and can really simplify string-processing programs.

Syntax

In the same way that strings are written between quotes, regular expression patterns are written between slashes (/). The search method of strings works like `indexOf`—it returns the position at which it finds its argument—but takes a regular expression instead of a string:

```
"doubledare".search(/le/);
→ 4
```

Since a slash normally indicates the end of the regular expression, slashes inside the expression have to be escaped with backslashes (but quotes do not). For example, here we define a regular expression that contains only a slash:

```
var slash = /\//;
"AC/DC".search(slash);
→ 2
```

Patterns specified by a regular expressions can do a few things that strings cannot do. For example, they allow some of their elements to match more than a single character.

Matching Sets of Characters

In Chapter 5, when extracting markup from a document, we needed to find the first asterisk or opening brace in a string. We could have done that with a regular expression, like this:

```
var asteriskOrBrace = /[\{\*]/;
var story = "We noticed the *giant sloth*, hanging from a giant branch.";
story.search(asteriskOrBrace);
→ 15
```

The [and] characters have a special meaning inside a regular expression. They enclose a list of characters and will match when one of these characters is found. Most punctuation characters have some special meaning inside a regular expression, so it is a good idea to always escape them with a backslash[1] when you use them to refer to the actual characters.

There are a few characters that actually refer to whole sets of characters within a regular expression. The dot (.) can be used to mean "any character that is not a line-break character." An escaped *d* (\d) means "any digit." An escaped *w* (\w) matches any "word" character, meaning alphabetic characters, digits, and the underscore character. An escaped *s* (\s) matches any whitespace character (things such as tabs, newlines, and spaces).

```
var digitSurroundedBySpace = /\s\d\s/;
"1a 2 3d".search(digitSurroundedBySpace);
→ 2
```

---

[1] In this case, the backslashes were not really necessary, because the characters occur between [and], where different rules apply. For now, it is easier to just escape them anyway so you won't have to think about it.

You can replace the \d, \w, and s\ characters with capital letters to negate their meanings. For example, \S matches any character that is *not* whitespace. When using [and], a pattern can be inverted by starting with a ^ character:

```
var notABC = /[^ABC]/;
"ABCBACCBBADABC".search(notABC);
→ 10
```

With what we know now, we can write a regular expression that matches a date in the format XX/XX/XXXX, where the Xs are digits—we had strings like that in Chapter 3: born 15/11/2003 (mother Spot): White Fang.

```
var datePattern = /\d\d\/\d\d\/\d\d\d\d/;
"born 15/11/2003 (mother Spot): White Fang".search(datePattern);
→ 5
```

The mass of backslashes makes the expression relatively hard to read. It says "digit, digit, slash, digit, digit, slash, digit, digit, digit, digit." In a moment, we'll see how to use a similar expression to actually extract the date from the string.

Matching Word and String Boundaries

Sometimes you need to make sure a pattern starts at the beginning of a string or ends at the string's end. You can use the special characters ^ and $ to do this. The ^ character matches the start of the string, and the $ character matches the end:

```
/a/.test("blah");
→ true
/^a$/.test("blah");
→ false
```

The first regular expression matches any string that contains an a character, while the second matches only the string "a". Note that regular expressions are objects and have methods. Their test method returns a Boolean indicating whether the given string matches the expression.

The \b escape character matches a "word boundary," which can be punctuation, whitespace, or the start or end of a string:

```
/cat/.test("concatenate");
→ true
/\bcat\b/.test("concatenate");
→ false
```

Repeating Patterns

It is possible to express the repeating of subpatterns in a regular expression. Putting an asterisk (*) after an element allows it to be repeated any number of times, including zero. A plus (+) does the same but requires the pattern to occur at least one time. A question mark (?) makes an element "optional"—it can occur zero or one time.

```
var parenthethicText = /\(.*\)/;
"Its (the sloth's) claws were gigantic!".search(parenthethicText);
→ 4
```

When necessary, you can use braces to specify the number of times an element may occur. A number between braces ({4}, for example) gives the exact number of times that element must occur. Two numbers with a comma between them ({3,10}) indicate that the pattern must occur at least as often as the first number and at most as often as the second one. Analogously, {2,} means two or more occurrences, while {,4} means four or less.

This is a more flexible pattern for matching dates:

```
var datePattern = /\d{1,2}\/\d\d?\/\d{4}/;
"born 15/11/2003 (mother Spot): White Fang".search(datePattern);
→ 5
```

The expressions /\d{1,2}/ and /\d\d?/ are two ways to express the same thing: "one or two digits."

Grouping Subexpressions

It is often necessary to use special characters like * or + on more than one character at a time. It is possible to group parts of a regular expression together with parentheses and then do something with the whole group. For example:

```
var cartoonCrying = /boo(hoo+)+/i;
cartoonCrying.test("Boohoooohoohooo");
→ true
```

The pattern hoo+ will match an h followed by two or more o characters. (hoo+)+ allows this pattern, as a whole, to be repeated one or more times.

Notice the i at the end of the regular expression. After the closing slash, "options" may be added to a regular expression. Here, the i means that the expression is case-insensitive, which allows the lowercase b in the pattern to match the uppercase B in the string. We'll see another option, g for "global," later on in this chapter.

Choosing Between Alternatives

For more advanced "branching" patterns, you can use a pipe character (|) to allow a pattern to make a choice between several elements. Here's an example:

```
var holyCow = /\b(sacred|holy) (cow|bovine|bull|taurus)\b/i;
holyCow.test("Sacred bovine!");
→ true
```

This will match any string that contains the word *sacred* or *holy*, followed by one of the words *cow, bovine, bull,* or *taurus*. Note that the parentheses are needed here, because otherwise the choice would be between *sacred, holy cow, bovine,* and so on.

Matching and Replacing

Often, looking for a pattern is just the first step in extracting something from a string. In previous chapters, such extraction was done by calling a string's indexOf and slice methods. Now that we know about regular expressions, we can do better.

The match Method

Strings have a method named match, which takes a regular expression as an argument. It returns null if the match failed and returns an array of matched strings if it succeeded. You can see this happen in the following examples:

```
"No".match(/yes/i);
→ null

"... yes".match(/yes/i);
→ ["yes"]

"Giant Ape".match(/giant (\w+)/i);
→ ["Giant Ape", "Ape"]
```

The first element in the returned array is always the part of the string that matched the whole pattern. As the third example shows, when there are parenthesized parts in the pattern, the parts they match are also added to the array. Often, this makes extracting pieces of a string very easy.

We can now rewrite the extractDate function that we wrote in Chapter 3. When given a string, this function looks for something that follows the date format we saw earlier. If it can find such a date, it puts the values into a Date object. Otherwise, it throws an exception.

```
function extractDate(string) {
  var found = string.match(/\b(\d\d?)\/(\d\d?)\/(\d{4})\b/);
  if (found == null)
    throw new Error("No date found in '" + string + "'.");
  return new Date(Number(found[3]), Number(found[2]) - 1, Number(found[1]));
}
```

This version of the function is no longer than the previous one, and it actually checks whether the input matches its expectations and shouts out when it is given nonsensical input. This was a lot harder without regular expressions—it would have taken a bunch of calls to indexOf to find out whether the numbers had one or two digits and whether the slashes were in the expected place.

Regular Expressions and the replace Method

The replace method of string values, which we saw in Chapter 5, can be given a regular expression as its first argument:

```
"Borobudur".replace(/[ou]/g, "a");
→ "Barabadar"
```

Notice the g character after the regular expression. It stands for "global" and means that every part of the string that matches the pattern should be replaced. When this g is omitted, only the first o would be replaced—this is a common mistake.

Sometimes we need to keep parts of the strings we replace. For example, say we have a big string containing the names of people, one name per line, in the format Lastname, Firstname. If we want to swap these names and remove the comma to get a simple Firstname Lastname format, we can use the following code:

```
var names = "Picasso, Pablo\nGauguin, Paul\nVan Gogh, Vincent";
names.replace(/([\w ]+), ([\w ]+)/g, "$2 $1");
→ "Pablo Picasso\nPaul Gauguin\nVincent Van Gogh"
```

The $1 and $2 in the replacement string refer to the parenthesized parts in the pattern. $1 is replaced by the text that matched against the first pair of parentheses, $2 by the second, and so on, up to $9.

If you have more than nine parenthetical parts in your pattern, this technique will no longer work. However, there is another even more flexible way to replace pieces of a string using regular expressions. When the second argument given to the replace method is a function value instead of a string, this function is called every time a match is found, and the matched text is replaced by whatever the function returns. The arguments given to the function are the matched elements, similar to the values found in the arrays returned by match: The first argument is the whole match, and after that there is an argument for every parenthesized part of the pattern.

Here's a simple example:

```
"the cia and fbi".replace(/\b(fbi|cia)\b/g, function(str) {
  return str.toUpperCase();
});
→ "the CIA and FBI"
```

And here's a cuter one:

```
var stock = "1 lemon, 2 cabbages, and 101 eggs";
function minusOne(match, amount, unit) {
  amount = Number(amount) - 1;
  if (amount == 1) // only one left, remove the 's'
    unit = unit.slice(0, unit.length - 1);
  else if (amount == 0)
    amount = "no";
  return amount + " " + unit;
}
stock.replace(/(\d+) (\w+)/g, minusOne);
→ "no lemon, 1 cabbage, and 100 eggs"
```

This takes a string, finds all occurrences of a number followed by an alphanumeric word, and returns a string wherein every such occurrence is decremented by one.

The (\d+) group ends up as the amount argument to the function, and the (\w+) group gets bound to unit. The function converts the amount to a number—which always works, since it matched \d+—and makes some adjustments in case there is only one or zero left.

This trick, passing a function to replace, can also be used to make the HTML-escaper from Chapter 5 more efficient. You may remember that it looked like this:

```
function escapeHTML(text) {
  var replacements = [["&", "&amp;"], ["\"", "&quot;"],
                      ["<", "&lt;"], [">", "&gt;"]];
  forEach(replacements, function(replace) {
    text = text.replace(replace[0], replace[1]);
  });
  return text;
}
```

We can now write a new version of escapeHTML that does the same thing but calls replace only once.

```
function escapeHTML(text) {
  var replacements = {"<": "&lt;", ">": "&gt;",
                      "&": "&amp;", "\"": "&quot;"};
  return text.replace(/[<>&"]/g, function(character) {
    return replacements[character];
  });
}
```

The replacements object is a quick way to associate each character with its escaped version. We could have used a Dictionary object from Chapter 6, since the object is used as to map values onto other values, but a simple object is also safe, because we know exactly which values will be used as properties and don't need the contains method (which checks whether a name is present in the object).

Dynamically Creating RegExp Objects

There are cases where you might not know the pattern you need to match against while you are writing the code. Say we are writing a (very simple-minded) obscenity filter for a message board, and we only want to allow messages that do not contain obscene words.

The most efficient way to check a piece of text for a set of words is to use a regular expression. Since we don't know in advance which words have to be in there, we have to create it in the code. For this, you use the RegExp constructor:

```
var badWords = ["ape", "monkey", "simian", "gorilla", "evolution"];
var pattern = new RegExp(badWords.join("|"), "i");
function isAcceptable(text) {
  return !pattern.test(text);
}

isAcceptable("The quick brown fox...");
→ true
isAcceptable("Cut that monkeybusiness out.");
→ false
isAcceptable("Mmmm, grapes.");
→ false
```

The first argument to the RegExp constructor is a string containing the pattern, and the second argument (which may be omitted) can be used to add case-insensitivity or globalness.

As an aside, we could add \b patterns around the words so that (for example) the "grapes" string would not be classified as unacceptable. However, that change would also make the "monkeybusiness" string acceptable, which is probably not correct. As you can see, obscenity filters are quite hard to get right (and usually just annoying).

When building a string to hold a regular expression pattern, you have to be careful with backslashes: Normally, backslashes are removed when a string is interpreted, so any backslashes that must end up in the regular expression itself have to be escaped:

```
var digits = new RegExp("\\d+");
```

Parsing an .ini File

Now let's look at a *real* problem that calls for regular expressions. Imagine we are writing a program to automatically harvest information about our enemies from the Internet. We will not actually write such a program here, just the part that reads the configuration file. This file looks like this:

```
searchengine=http://www.google.com/search?q=$1
spitefulness=9.7

; comments are preceded by a semicolon...
; these are sections, concerning individual enemies
[larry]
fullname=Larry Doe
type=kindergarten bully
website=http://www.geocities.com/CapeCanaveral/11451

[gargamel]
fullname=Gargamel
type=evil sorcerer
outputdir=/home/marijn/enemies/gargamel
```

The exact rules for this format (which is actually a widely used format, usually called an *.ini* file) are as follows:

- Blank lines and lines starting with semicolons are ignored.
- Lines wrapped in [and] start a new section.
- Lines containing an alphanumeric identifier followed by an = character add a setting to the current section.
- Anything else is invalid.

Our task is to convert a string like this into an array of objects, each with a name and an array of name/value pairs. We'll need one such object for each section and one for the section-less settings.

Since the format has to be processed line by line, splitting it up into separate lines is a good start. So far, we have always used string.split("\n") for this. Some operating systems, however, use not just a newline character to separate lines but a carriage return character followed by a newline ("\r\n").

Given that the split method of strings also allows a regular expression as its argument, the following function splits a string into an array of lines, allowing both "\n" and "\r\n" between lines.

```
function splitLines(string) {
  return string.split(/\r?\n/);
}
```

That gives us all we need to write our *.ini* file parsing function:

```
function parseINI(string) {
  var lines = splitLines(string);
  var categories = [];

  function newCategory(name) {
    var cat = {name: name, fields: []};
    categories.push(cat);
    return cat;
  }
  var currentCategory = newCategory("TOP");

  forEach(lines, function(line) {
    var match;
    if (/^\s*(;.*)?$/.test(line))
      return;
    else if (match = line.match(/^\[(.*)\]$/))
      currentCategory = newCategory(match[1]);
    else if (match = line.match(/^(\w+)=(.*)$/))
      currentCategory.fields.push({name: match[1], value: match[2]});
    else
      throw new Error("Line '" + line + "' is invalid.");
  });

  return categories;
}
```

In short, the code goes over every line in the file. It keeps a "current category" object, and when it finds a normal directive, it adds it to this object. When it encounters a line that starts a new category, it replaces the current category with a new one, to which subsequent directives will get added. Finally, it returns an array containing all the categories it came across.

Note the recurring use of ^ and $ to make sure the expression matches the whole line, not just part of it. Leaving these out is a common mistake, which results in code that mostly works but behaves strangely for some input.

The expression /^\s*(;.*)?$/ can be used to test for lines that can be ignored. Do you see how it works? The part between the parentheses will match comments, and the ? after that will make sure it also matches lines of whitespace.

The pattern if (match = string.match(...)) is something you'll commonly see when using regular expressions. You typically aren't completely sure that your expression will match and you do not want your code to try to evaluate something like null[1], so you need to test whether match returns a non-null value. To not break the elegant chain of if forms, you can assign this result to a variable as the test for if and do the matching and the testing in a single line.

Conclusion

Right now, the most important thing to know about regular expressions is that they exist and can make your string-mangling code much shorter. In fact, there is quite a lot more to learn about regular expressions than the material found in this chapter. Look around on the Internet, if you feel like it—the syntax used by JavaScript's regular expressions is called Perl Compatible Regular Expressions and is found in a lot of other programming languages as well.

This syntax is so cryptic that you'll probably have to go look up the details the first 10 or so times you need to use it. Persevere, and you will soon be writing brilliantly complicated, occult-looking expressions.

9

WEB PROGRAMMING: A CRASH COURSE

This chapter contains a quick introduction to the various elements that make the Web work and the way they relate to JavaScript. The three chapters after this one are more practical and show some of the ways JavaScript can be used to inspect and change a web page.

The Internet

Basically, the Internet is a computer network spanning most of the world. A computer network makes it possible for computers to send each other messages. The techniques underlying networking are very interesting, but are not the subject of this book. All you have to know is that, typically, one computer, which we will call the *server*, is waiting for other computers to start talking to it. Once another computer, the *client*, opens communications with this server, they are able to send each other data. In order for both parties to understand each other, this data transfer must be guided by some *protocol*, or convention for communication.

The Internet is used to carry messages for many different protocols. There are protocols for chatting, protocols for file sharing, protocols used by malicious software to control the computer of the poor schmuck who got infected, and so on. The protocol that is of interest to us is the one used by the World Wide Web. It is called *HTTP*, which stands for HyperText Transfer Protocol, and is used to retrieve web pages and the files associated with them.

In HTTP communication, the server is the computer on which the web page is stored. The client is the computer that asks the server for a page so that it can display it. Asking for a page like this is called an *HTTP request*.

URLs

Web pages and other resources that are accessible through the Internet are identified by *URLs*, which stands for Universal Resource Locators. A URL looks like this:

```
http://acc6.its.brooklyn.cuny.edu/~phalsall/texts/taote-v3.html
```

It is composed of three parts. The first part, `http://`, indicates that this URL uses the HTTP protocol. There are some other protocols, such as File Transfer Protocol (FTP) and Secure HTTP (HTTPS), which also make use of URLs. The next part, `acc6.its.brooklyn.cuny.edu`, names the server on which this page can be found. The final part of the URL, `/~phalsal/texts/taote-v3.html`, names a specific file on this server.

The usual way to access the World Wide Web is through a browser. After typing in a URL or clicking a link, the browser makes an HTTP request to the appropriate server. If all goes well, the server responds by sending a file back to the browser, which in turn shows it to the user (in one way or another).

When, as in the example, the retrieved file is an HTML document, it will be displayed as a web page. We briefly discussed HTML in Chapter 5, where we saw that it could contain styling information and refer to image files. In Chapter 7, I mentioned that HTML pages can also contain `<script>` tags to load files of JavaScript code. When showing an HTML document, a browser will automatically fetch all the script and image files that the page uses so that it can add them to the document.

Server-Side Programming

Although a URL often points to a concrete file, it is possible for a web server to do something more complicated than just looking up a file and sending it to the client. It could, for example, somehow preprocess this file first. Or maybe there is no file at all, but only a program that, given a URL, has some way of generating a document for it.

Programs that transform or generate documents allow us to make more advanced web pages. A file is just a file, static and noninteractive. But when there is a program being executed for every request, the resulting page can be customized for each particular user, based on things like whether they have logged in or specified certain preferences. This can also make managing the content of web pages much easier—instead of adding a new HTML file whenever something new is put on a website, a new document is added to some central storage (usually a database system), and the program that creates the web pages finds it there and knows how to show it to clients.

This kind of web programming is called *server-side programming*. It affects the document before it is sent to the user. In some cases, it is also useful to have a program that runs *after* the page has been sent, when the user is looking at it. This is called *client-side programming*, because the program runs on the client's computer. Client-side web programming is what JavaScript was invented for.

Client-Side Programming

Running programs on the client side is inherently problematic. You can never really know in advance what kinds of programs the page you are visiting is going to run. If it can send information from your computer to others, damage something, or infiltrate your system, surfing the Web would be dangerous.

To work around this issue, browsers severely limit the things a JavaScript program may do. It is not allowed to look at the files on your computer or to modify anything not related to the web page it was embedded in. Isolating a programming environment like this is called *sandboxing*. Allowing the programs enough room to be useful but at the same time restricting them enough to make them harmless is not an easy thing to do. Every few months some JavaScript programmer comes up with a new way to circumvent the limitations and do something harmful or privacy-invading. The people responsible for the browsers respond by modifying their programs to make this trick impossible, and all is well again—until the next problem is discovered.

Basic Web Scripting

We will now walk through some of the things that a JavaScript environment in a web browser provides and look at some simple things that can be done with client-side programming.

The window Object

One of the first widespread uses of JavaScript was the open method of the window object. It takes a URL as an argument and will open a new window showing that URL.

```
var comicwindow = window.open("http://www.pbfcomics.com");
```

If you try that nowadays, your browser will probably block the new window from opening. Web programmers, especially those trying to get people to pay attention to advertisements, have abused this `window.open` method so much that by now, it is considered really bad style and not allowed by default. It still has its uses, but as a general rule, your scripts should not open any new windows unless the user asked for them.

Note that, because `open` is a method on the `window` object, the `window.` part can be left off. When a function is called "normally," it is called as a method on the top-level object, which is what `window` is. Personally, I think `open` sounds a bit generic, so I usually use `window.open`, which makes it clear that it is a window that is being opened.

The value returned by `window.open` is a new window. This is the global object for the script running in that window, and it contains all the standard things like the `Object` constructor and the `Math` object. But if you try to look at them, most browsers will (probably) not let you—they will trigger some form of security exception instead.

This is part of the sandboxing that I mentioned earlier. Pages opened by your browser might show information that is meant only for you (if you open, for example, the website of your bank and log in). It would be bad if any random script running on another web page could mess with them. The exception to this rule is pages opened on the same domain: When a script running on a page from eloquentjavascript.net opens another page on that same domain, it can do everything it wants to this page.

An opened window can be closed with its `close` method. Here's an example:

```
comicwindow.close();
```

Other kinds of subdocuments, such as frames (documents within a document), are also windows from the perspective of a JavaScript program and have their own `window` object and JavaScript environment.

The document Object

Every window object has a `document` property, which contains an object representing the document shown in that window. This object contains, for example, a property `location`, with information about the URL of the document.

```
document.location.href;
→ "http://eloquentjavascript.net/chapter10.html"
```

Setting `document.location.href` to a new URL can be used to make the browser load another document. Another application of the `document` object is its `write` method. This method, when given a string argument, writes some HTML to the document. When it is used on a fully loaded document, it will replace the whole document by the given HTML, which is usually not what you intended. The way to use this function is to have a script call it while the document is being loaded, in which case the written HTML will be inserted into the document at the place of the script tag that triggered it. This is a simple way to add some dynamic elements to a page. For example, here is a simple document showing the current time:

```html
<html>
  <head><title>The time</title></head>
  <body>
    <h1>The time</h1>
    <p>The time is
      <script type="text/javascript">
        var time = new Date();
        document.write(time.getHours() + ":" + time.getMinutes());
      </script>
    </p>
  </body>
</html>
```

Often, the techniques we'll discuss in Chapter 10 provide a cleaner and more versatile way to modify the document, but for simple things, document.write works well.

Timers

The window object also provides methods for scheduling things to happen after a certain amount of time. If we have, for example, a web page that allows the user to make a choice between two links (/spoiler.html and /nospoiler.html) and that automatically picks the most likely link after five seconds, the page could look like this:

```html
<html>
  <head><title>Spoiler alert!</title></head>
  <body>
    <p>The following page might include spoilers! Continue?</p>
    <p><a href="/spoiler.html">Yes</a> (or wait five seconds)</p>
    <p><a href="/nospoiler.html">No!</a></p>
    <script type="text/javascript">
      window.setTimeout(function() {
        document.location.href = "/spoiler.html";
      }, 5000);
    </script>
  </body>
</html>
```

The script at the bottom of the document tag calls window.setTimeout, which "schedules" its first argument to be called after the amount of milliseconds (1/1000 second) given as the second argument. The first argument can be either a function, which will be called, or a string containing a JavaScript program, which will be executed.

A timeout can be canceled by passing the value that setTimeout returns (which we ignore in the example) to window.clearTimeout.

There are similar functions for repeated time-based actions. window.setInterval causes a function or string to be executed repeatedly, with the amount of milliseconds between calls specified as a second argument. window.clearInterval can be used to stop such an effect.

Forms

Another popular application of JavaScript in web pages centers around *forms*. In case you aren't familiar with forms, let me give a quick summary.

A basic HTTP request is a simple request for a file. When this file is not really a passive file but a server-side program, it can be useful to include information other than a filename in the request. For this purpose, URLs are allowed to contain additional "parameters," such as these:

```
http://www.google.com/search?q=aztec%20empire
```

After the filename (/search), the URL continues with a question mark, after which the parameters follow. This request has a single parameter, called q (for "query," presumably), whose value is aztec empire. The %20 part corresponds to a space. There are a number of characters that are not allowed in these parameters, such as spaces, ampersands, or the equals sign. These are "escaped" (similar to the way backslashes are used in strings) by replacing them with a % followed by their numerical value in hexadecimal form. If that doesn't mean anything to you, don't worry—we'll use built-in functions that do the encoding and decoding for us.

JavaScript provides the encodeURIComponent and decodeURIComponent functions to do this escaping and to undo it again:

```
var encoded = encodeURIComponent("aztec empire");
encoded;
→ "aztec%20empire"
decodeURIComponent(encoded);
→ "aztec empire"
```

When a request contains more than one parameter, they are separated by ampersands, like this:

```
http://www.google.com/search?q=aztec%20empire&lang=nl
```

Basically, a form is a way to make it easy for browser users to create such parametrized URLs. It contains a number of fields, such as input boxes for text, check boxes, or widgets that allow you to choose from a given set of values. It also usually contains a "submit" button and, invisible to the user, an "action" URL to which the data should be sent. When the submit button is clicked, or ENTER is pressed, the information that was entered in the fields is added to this action URL as parameters, and the browser will request this URL.

Here is the HTML for a simple form:

```
<form name="userinfo" method="get" action="/info.html">
  <p>Please give us your information, so that we can send
  you spam.</p>
  <p>Name: <input type="text" name="name"></p>
  <p>Email: <input type="text" name="email"></p>
  <p>Sex: <select name="sex">
          <option>Won't say</option>
          <option>Male</option>
          <option>Female</option>
        </select></p>
  <p><input name="send" type="submit" value="Send!"></p>
</form>
```

In a browser, this form might look like this:

Please give us your information, so that we can send you spam.

Name:

E-Mail:

Sex: Won't say ·

Send!

The name of the form can be used to access it with JavaScript, as we shall see in a moment. The names of the fields determine the names of the HTTP parameters that are used to store their values. Sending this form might produce a URL like this:

```
http://planetspam.com/info.html?name=Ted&email=ted@zork.com&sex=Male
```

This assumes that the page showing the form was shown on the *planetspam.com* server. When a URL does not contain an *http://* part and a server name, such as the URL */info.html* used as the form's action, it is called a *relative URL*. Relative URLs are interpreted by the browser to refer to files on the same server as the current document. When they do not start with a slash, the path (or directory) of the current document is also retained, and the given path is appended to it. For example, the relative URL *manual.html*, when used from the page at *http://test.org/test/index.html*, will result in *http://test.org/test/manual.html*.

The `method="get"` property of the example form shown previously indicates that this form should encode the values it is given as URL parameters, as shown earlier. There is an alternative method for sending parameters, which is called post. An HTTP request using the post method contains, in addition to a URL, a block of data. A form using the post method puts the values of its parameters in this data block instead of in the URL.

When sending big chunks of data, the get method will result in URLs that are a mile wide, so post is usually more convenient. But the difference between the two methods is not just a question of convenience. Traditionally, get requests are used for requests that just ask the server for some document, while post requests are used to take an action that changes something on the server. For example, getting a list of recent messages on an Internet forum would be a get request, while adding a new message would be a post request. There is a good reason why most pages follow this distinction—programs that automatically explore the Web, such as those used by search engines, will generally only make get requests. If changes to a site can be made by get requests, these well-meaning "crawlers" could do all kinds of damage.

Scripting a Form

When the browser is displaying a page containing a form, JavaScript programs can inspect and modify the values that are entered in the form's fields. This opens up possibilities for all kinds of neat tricks, such as checking values before they are sent to the server or automatically filling in certain fields.

We will be adding a validity check to the form shown earlier so that it submits only if the name field is not left empty, and the email field contains something that looks like a halfway valid email address. Because we no longer want the form to submit immediately when the Send! button is clicked, we need to change its type property from `"submit"` to `"button"`, which will turn it into a regular button with no effect. (Chapter 11 will show a *much* better way of doing this.)

```
<input name="send" type="button" value="Send!">
```

Every HTML tag shown in a document has a JavaScript object associated with it. These objects can be used to inspect and manipulate almost every aspect of the document. In this chapter, we're only working with the objects for forms and form fields. In Chapter 10 we'll talk about these objects in general.

The document object has a property named forms, which contains links to all the forms in the document, by name. Our form has a property `name="userinfo"`, so it can be found under the property userinfo.

```
var spamForm = document.forms.userinfo;
spamForm.method;
→ "get"
```

```
spamForm.action;
→ "/info.html"
```

In this case, the properties method and action that were given to the HTML form tag are also present as properties of the JavaScript object. This is usually the case, but not always—some HTML properties are spelled differently in JavaScript, and others are not present at all. Chapter 10 will show a way to get at all properties.

Next, we will want to get at the actual fields of the form. The object for the form tag has a property elements, which refers to an object containing the fields of the form, by name. The following code would put the name "Eugène" in the form's name field:

```
spamForm.elements.name.value = "Eugène";
```

Text-input objects have a value property, which can be used to read and change their content.

With what we know now, we can write a function that takes a form object as its argument and returns a Boolean value: true when the name field is not empty and when the email field contains something that matches a regular expression (see Chapter 8) made to recognize email addresses, and false otherwise:

```
function validInfo(form) {
  return form.elements.name.value != "" &&
    /^.+@.+\.\w{2,4}$/.test(form.elements.email.value);
}
```

All we have to do now is determine what happens when people click the Send! button. At the moment (having changed its type attribute from "submit" to "button"), it does not do anything at all. This can be remedied by setting its onclick property to a JavaScript function:

```
spamForm.elements.send.onclick = function() {
  if (validInfo(spamForm))
    spamForm.submit();
  else
    alert("Give us a name and a valid email address!");
};
```

Just like the actions given to setInterval and setTimeout, the value stored in an onclick (or similar) property can be either a function or a string of JavaScript code. In this case, we give it a function. Now, when the button is clicked, the form's validity is checked. If the form is valid, it is submitted to the server (which is what the submit method does); otherwise, an error message appears.

Autofocus

Another trick related to form inputs, as well as other things that can be "selected," such as buttons and links, is the focus method. When you know for sure that a user will want to start typing in a certain text field as soon as he enters the page, you can have your script start by placing the cursor in it so he won't have to click it or select it in some other way:

```
spamForm.elements.name.focus();
```

Some pages also automatically make the cursor jump to the next field when it looks like you finished filling in one field—for example, when you type a ZIP code. This should not be overdone—it makes the page behave in a way the user does not expect. If he is used to pressing Tab to move the cursor manually or mistyped the last character and wants to remove it, such magic cursor-jumping is only annoying.

Browser Incompatibility

So, that all looks easy. But let me assure you, client-side web programming isn't always that straightforward—it can, at times, be a painful ordeal. Why? Because there are different systems that interpret client-side programs (different browsers mostly), and these tend to behave in slightly different ways. You'll usually want your program to work for all popular browsers, but the only way to be sure that it does is to test it in all of them and work around any problems you encounter.

On the bright side, things have gotten much, much better in this regard in the past years. The *really* broken browsers (Netscape 4, Internet Explorer 5) have become extinct, Internet Explorer 6 is also on the way out, and the latest releases of all major browsers (Opera, Firefox, Safari, Chrome, and Internet Explorer) are of a much better quality.

Unfortunately, even these new browsers all still contain several bugs (programming errors), which often take a long time to get fixed. But do not let that discourage you. With the right kind of obsessive-compulsive mindset, such problems provide wonderful challenges. And for those of us who do not like wasting our time on things like that, carefully avoiding the obscure corners of the browser's functionality will generally prevent you from running into too much trouble.

Bugs aside, the intentional, by-design differences between browsers don't make our life easy either. The current situation looks something like this: On one hand, there are all the "new" browsers: Firefox, Safari, Chrome, and Opera are the most important ones, but there are more. These browsers all make a reasonable effort to adhere to a set of standards that have been developed, or are being developed, by the W3C and WHATWG, organizations that try to make the Web a less confusing place by defining standard interfaces for all the functionality provided by browsers. On the other hand, there is Internet Explorer, Microsoft's browser, which rose to dominance in a time when many of these standards did not really exist yet and hasn't made much effort to adjust itself to what other people are doing.

In some areas, such as the way the content of an HTML document can be approached from JavaScript (Chapter 10), the standards are based on the method that Internet Explorer invented, and things work more or less the same on all browsers. In other areas, such as the way events (mouse clicks, key presses, and such) are handled (Chapter 11), Internet Explorer works radically differently from other browsers.

For a long time, owing partially to the cluelessness of the average Java-Script developer and partially to the fact that browser incompatibilities were much worse when browsers like Internet Explorer version 4 or 5 and old versions of Netscape were still common, the usual way to deal with such differences was to detect which browser the user was running and litter the code with alternate solutions for each browser—if we are running in Internet Explorer, do this; if we have Netscape, do that; and if this is another browser that we didn't think of, just hope for the best. You can imagine how hideous, confusing, and long such programs were.

Many sites would also just refuse to load when opened in a browser that was "not supported." This caused a few of the minor browsers to swallow their pride and pretend they were Internet Explorer, just so they would be allowed to load such pages.

The navigator object was originally introduced as a place for browser-specific functionality. Various browsers put different properties in there, most of them providing information about the browser and the platform it is running on. On my version of Chrome, the following is shown:

```
navigator.userAgent;
→ "Mozilla/5.0 (X11; U; Linux x86_64; en-US) AppleWebKit/532.9\
   (KHTML, like Gecko) Chrome/5.0.307.11 Safari/532.9"
navigator.vendor;
→ "Google Inc."
navigator.platform;
→ "Linux i686"
```

Given this, a program could look for the string Chrome/ in navigator.userAgent, and run some Chrome-specific code if it was found.

A better approach is to try to "isolate" our programs from differences in browsers. For example, if you need to find out more about an event, such as the clicks we handled by setting the onclick property of our send button, you have to look at the top-level object called event on Internet Explorer, but you have to use the first argument passed to the event-handling function on other browsers. To handle this and a number of other differences related to events, you can write a helper function for attaching events to things, which takes care of all the plumbing and allows the event-handling functions themselves to be the same for all browsers. In Chapter 11 we will write such a function.

NOTE *The browser quirks mentioned in the following chapters refer to the state of affairs in early 2010 and might no longer be accurate on some points.*

It is important to note that there is a group of web users who browse the Internet without JavaScript. A lot of people use a regular graphical browser with JavaScript disabled for security reasons. Then there are people using textual browsers, or browsers for blind people. When working on a "serious" site, it is a good idea to start with a plain HTML system that works and then add nonessential tricks and conveniences with JavaScript.

Further Reading

These chapters will only give a somewhat superficial introduction to the subject of browser interfaces. They are not the main subject of this book, and they are complex enough to fill a thick book on their own. When you understand the basics of these interfaces (and understand something about HTML), it is not too hard to look for specific information online. The interface documentation for the Firefox and Internet Explorer browsers are a good way to start:

*   *http://www.mozilla.org/docs/dom/domref/dom_shortTOC.html*
*   *http://msdn2.microsoft.com/library/yek4tbz0.aspx*

10

THE DOCUMENT OBJECT MODEL

In Chapter 9 we saw JavaScript objects that represented the form and input tags from an HTML document. Such objects are part of a structure called the *Document Object Model* (DOM). Every tag in the document is represented by an object in this model and can be looked up and interacted with.

DOM Elements

HTML documents have a hierarchical structure. Each element (tag) except the top <html> element is contained in another element, called its *parent*. This element can in turn contain *child* elements. You can visualize this as a kind of family tree. If we have a simple document like this:

```
<html>
  <head>
    <title>Alchemy for beginners</title>
    <script type="text/javascript" src="js/base.js"></script>
  </head>
```

```
<body>
  <h1>Chapter 1: Equipment</h1>
  <p>This is what an <em>alchemists' bottle</em> looks like:</p>
  <img src="img/florence_flask.png" alt="a fat bottle" id="picture">
</body>
</html>
```

then the tree would look like this:

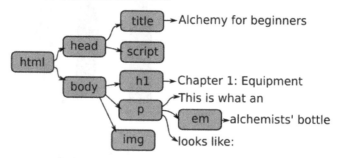

The document object model is based on such a view of the document. Note that the tree contains two types of elements: nodes, which are shown as boxes, and pieces of simple text. The pieces of text, as we will see, work somewhat differently than the other elements. For one thing, they never have children.

The object for the root of the document tree, the html node, can be reached through the documentElement property of the document object. However, most of the time we need access to the body element, rather than the root. This can be found under document.body.

Node Links

The links between these nodes are available as properties of the node objects. Every DOM object has a parentNode property, which refers to the object in which it is contained, if any. These parents also have links pointing back to their children, but because there can be more than one child, these are stored in a pseudoarray called childNodes. In the document shown in the diagram, document.body.childNodes contains three elements: an h1 header element, a paragraph, and an image.

For convenience, there are also links called firstChild and lastChild, pointing at the first and last children inside a node, or null when there are no children.

Finally, there are properties called nextSibling and previousSibling, which point at the nodes sitting "next" to a node—nodes that are children of the same parent, coming before or after the current node. Again, when there is no such sibling, the value of these properties is null. For example, the h1 element in the example document has a previousSibling property of null and a nextSibling property that points at the paragraph element.

Types of Nodes

To find out whether a node represents a simple piece of text or an actual HTML node, we can look at its `nodeType` property. This contains a number, 1 for regular nodes and 3 for text nodes.

```
function isTextNode(node) {
  return node.nodeType == 3;
}
```

```
isTextNode(document.body);
→ false
isTextNode(document.body.firstChild.firstChild);
→ true
```

There are 12 such node types, used for various aspects of the DOM tree. (For example, the `document` object has a node type of 9.) However, apart from allowing us to distinguish text nodes, these types serve very little use in JavaScript. The reason that the DOM interface sometimes seems needlessly obscure and cumbersome is that it is specified as an interface that can be implemented in any programming language, not just JavaScript.

Regular (nontext) nodes have a property called `nodeName`, indicating the type of HTML tag that they represent. Text nodes, on the other hand, have a `nodeValue`, containing their text content.

```
document.body.firstChild.nodeName;
→ "H1"
document.body.firstChild.firstChild.nodeValue;
→ "Chapter 1: Equipment"
```

The node names are always capitalized, which is something you need to take into account if you ever want to compare them to something, as in the following function:

```
function isImage(node) {
  return !isTextNode(node) && node.nodeName == "IMG";
}
```

```
isImage(document.body.lastChild);
→ true
```

The innerHTML Property

Each node object has an `innerHTML` property, which represents the HTML text *inside* of the node. You can read it but also set it to a new value. Doing this, for example, would replace the body of your document with a single paragraph:

```
document.body.innerHTML = "<p>Oops</p>";
```

Similarly, the `nodeValue` of a text node can be set to a new value in order to change the text content. Note that, with `innerHTML`, the given string is interpreted as HTML, while with `nodeValue` it is interpreted as plain text, so angle brackets do not have a special meaning.

Finding Your Node

In a few of the examples, I have been finding nodes in the document by going through a series of `firstChild` and `lastChild` properties. This can work, but it is verbose and easy to break—if we add another node at the start of our document, `document.body.firstChild` no longer refers to the h1 element, and code that assumes it does is broken. On top of that, some browsers will add text nodes for things like spaces and newlines between tags, while others do not, so the exact layout of the DOM tree can vary.

A better way to do this is to give elements that you need to have access to an id attribute. In the example document, the picture has the ID `"picture"`. We can use this to look it up:

```
var picture = document.getElementById("picture");
picture.src;
→ "img/florence_flask.png"
picture.src = "img/ostrich.png";
```

The `getElementById` method of the `document` object takes an ID string and returns the node that has this `id`, or `null` when no such node is found. When typing `getElementById`, note that the last letter is lowercase.

The last line in the previous code, which changes `picture.src`, will actually cause the picture shown in the document to change. Almost every aspect of an HTML document can be changed in this way—finding the node we need and manipulating its attributes or child-node relations.

DOM nodes also have a method `getElementsByTagName` that, when given a tag name, returns an array of all nodes of that type contained in the node it was called on. For example, in our example document, `document.body` `.getElementsByTagName("EM")[0]` will return the element for `<em>alchemists' bottle</em>`.

Node Creation

Another thing we can do with these DOM nodes is to create new ones ourselves. This makes it possible to add to a document at will. Unfortunately, the interface for doing this is somewhat clumsy.

The `document` object has `createElement` and `createTextNode` methods. The first is used to create regular nodes; the second, as the name suggests, creates text nodes. Let's create one of both:

```
var secondHeader = document.createElement("H1");
var secondTitle = document.createTextNode("Chapter 2: Deep magic");
```

Next, we'll want to put the title name into the h1 element and then add the element to the document. The simplest way to do this is the appendChild method, which can be called on (nontext) nodes. This will put the text into the header and add the header to the document:

```
secondHeader.appendChild(secondTitle);
document.body.appendChild(secondHeader);
```

Often, you will also want to give these new nodes some attributes. For example, an img (image) tag is rather useless without an src property telling the browser which image it should show. Most attributes can be approached directly as properties of the DOM nodes, but there are also methods setAttribute and getAttribute, which are used to access attributes in a more general way:

```
var newImage = document.createElement("IMG");
newImage.setAttribute("src", "img/yinyang.png");
document.body.appendChild(newImage);
newImage.getAttribute("src");
→ "img/yinyang.png"
```

A Creation Helper Function

When we want to build more than a few simple nodes, it gets very tiresome to create every single node with a call to document.createElement or document .createTextNode and then add its attributes and child nodes one by one. Fortunately, it is not hard to write a function to do most of the work for us:

```
function dom(name, attributes /*, children...*/) {
  var node = document.createElement(name);
  if (attributes) {
    forEachIn(attributes, function(name, value) {
      node.setAttribute(name, value);
    });
  }
  for (var i = 2; i < arguments.length; i++) {
    var child = arguments[i];
    if (typeof child == "string")
      child = document.createTextNode(child);
    node.appendChild(child);
  }
  return node;
}
```

This function creates a node of the type given as its first argument, sets its attributes based on the properties of the second argument (if given), and then adds any remaining arguments as children of the new node, converting strings to text nodes first. This is how it could be used to add another paragraph to our document:

```
document.body.appendChild(
  dom("P", null, "A paragraph with a ",
      dom("A", {href: "http://en.wikipedia.org/wiki/Alchemy"}, "link"),
      " inside of it."));
```

Moving Nodes Around

appendChild is not the only way nodes can be inserted into another node. When the new node should not appear at the end of its parent, the insertBefore method can be used to place it in front of another child node. It takes the new node as a first argument and the existing child as a second argument.

If a node that already has a parentNode is placed somewhere, it is automatically removed from its current position—nodes cannot exist in the document in more than one place.

When a node must be replaced by another one, use the replaceChild method, which again takes the new node as a first argument and the existing one as a second argument.

And, finally, there is removeChild to remove a child node. Note that this is called on the *parent* of the node to be removed, giving the child as an argument.

All three functions discussed earlier require redundant information to be provided—they are methods on the parent node and take a child node of this parent as one of the arguments. You'll often need to do things like this:

```
node.parentNode.removeChild(node);
```

If you do not like repeating yourself, you can define shorthands like this:

```
function removeNode(node) {
  node.parentNode.removeChild(node);
}
function insertBefore(newNode, node) {
  node.parentNode.insertBefore(newNode, node);
}
```

When creating new nodes and moving nodes around, it is necessary to be aware of the following rule: Nodes are not allowed to be inserted into another document from the one in which they were created. This means that if you have extra frames or windows open, you cannot take a piece of the document from one and move it to another, and nodes created with methods on one document object must stay in that document. Some browsers, notably Firefox, do not enforce this restriction, so a program that violates it will work fine in those browsers but break in others.

An Implementation of print

An example of something useful that can be done by manipulating the document is an implementation of the print function we have been using throughout the book:

```
var output = dom("DIV", {id: "printOutput"}, dom("H1", null, "Print output:"));
document.body.appendChild(output);

function print() {
  var result = [];
  forEach(arguments, function(arg){result.push(String(arg));});
  output.appendChild(dom("PRE", null, result.join("")));
}
```

The code first creates a div element, which is a generic container-type element, for print to put its text in. It gives this element an id to make it easy to find and to style (styling will be discussed in a moment) and puts a header on top of it. The print function simply puts all its arguments into a big string (remember that it allowed multiple arguments to be passed) and adds a pre element containing this text to the output area.

pre stands for preformatted, which means newlines and spacing in such an element will be preserved. In other elements, newlines are treated as if they were spaces, and multiple subsequent spaces (or tabs or other whitespace) are treated as a single space. This is convenient when writing HTML, since we can break our lines where we want and still have the text flow properly in the resulting document. But when having a program output text, we probably want all characters to be preserved.

Style Sheets

Closely tied to HTML and the DOM is the topic of *style sheets*. It is a big topic, and I will not discuss it entirely, but some understanding of style sheets is necessary for a lot of interesting JavaScript techniques.

In old-fashioned HTML, the only way to change the appearance of elements in a document was to give them extra attributes or to wrap them in extra tags, such as center to center them horizontally or font to change the font style or color. This meant that if you wanted the paragraphs or the headers in your document to look a certain way, you had to add a bunch of attributes and tags to *every single one of them*. This quickly adds a lot of noise to such documents and makes them annoying to write or to change.

Well, people are inventive, and someone came up with a solution for this problem. Style sheets are a way to make statements like "in this document, all paragraphs should use the Comic Sans font and should be purple; all tables should have a thick green border." You specify them once, at the top of the document or in a separate file, and they affect the whole document. Here, for example, is a style sheet to make headers 22 points big and centered and to make paragraphs use the font and color mentioned earlier when they have a class attribute of "ugly":

```
<style type="text/css">
  h1 {
    font-size: 22pt;
    text-align: center;
  }
  p.ugly {
    font-family: Comic Sans MS;
    color: purple;
  }
</style>
```

Classes are a concept related to styles. If you have different kinds of paragraphs, say ugly ones and pretty ones, setting the style for all p elements is not what you want, so *classes* can be used to distinguish between them. The previous style will only be applied to paragraphs like this:

```
<p class="ugly">Mirror, mirror...</p>
```

In DOM node objects, you'll find a className property corresponding to the class attribute. The word class couldn't be used since (as was mentioned in Chapter 1) that is a reserved word in JavaScript.

The style Property

There is much more to styles: Some styles are inherited by child nodes from parent nodes and interfere with each other in complex and interesting ways. For the purpose of DOM programming, the most important things to know are that each DOM node has a style property, which can be used to manipulate the style of that node, and that there are a few kinds of styles that can be used to make nodes do extraordinary things.

This style property refers to an object, which has properties for all the possible elements of the style. We can, for example, give the picture in our document a border 4 pixels wide:

```
picture.style.borderWidth = "4px";
```

Note that in style sheets, the words are separated by hyphens, as in border-width, while in JavaScript, capital letters are used to mark the different words, as in borderWidth.

Hiding Nodes

A very useful styling is display: none. This can be used to temporarily hide a node: When style.display is "none", the element does not appear at all to the viewer of the document, even though it still exists. Later, display can be set to the empty string, and the element will reappear.

```
picture.style.display = "none";
// picture gone
picture.style.display = "";
// picture visible again
```

Positioning

Another set of style types that can be abused in interesting ways are those related to positioning. In a simple HTML document, the browser takes care of determining the screen positions of all the elements—each element is put next to or below the elements that come before it, and nodes (generally) do not overlap.

When its position style is set to "absolute", a node is taken out of the normal document "flow." It no longer takes up room in the document but sort of floats above it. The left and top styles can then be used to influence its position. This can be used for various purposes, from making a node obnoxiously follow the mouse cursor to making "windows" open on top of the rest of the document. This would make our picture spin around the document in circles:

```
picture.style.position = "absolute";
var angle = 0;
setInterval(function() {
  angle += 0.1;
  picture.style.left = (100 + 100 * Math.cos(angle)) + "px";
  picture.style.top = (100 + 100 * Math.sin(angle)) + "px";
}, 100);
```

If you aren't familiar with trigonometry, just believe me when I tell you that the cosine and sine stuff is used to build coordinates lying on the outline of a circle. Ten times per second, the angle at which we place the picture is changed, and new coordinates are computed.

It is a common error when setting styles like this to forget to append "px" to your value. In most cases, setting a style to a number without a unit does not work, so you must add "px" for pixels, "%" for percent, "em" for "ems" (the width of an "M" character), or "pt" for points.

The place that is treated as 0,0 for the purpose of these positions depends on the place of the node in the document. When it is placed inside another node that has position: absolute or position: relative, the top left of this node is used. Otherwise, you get the top-left corner of the document.

Controlling Node Size

There are also width and height styles, which are used to determine the size of an element. This, for example, would force the picture element to be 400 by 200 pixels in size:

```
picture.style.width = "400px";
picture.style.height = "200px";
```

Word of Caution

The tricks shown in this chapter, especially when combined with those from the next chapter, allow you to more or less redefine the way the browser works. With great power comes great responsibility. It can be tempting to add all kinds of bling-bling and custom behavior to a page, but keep in mind that people expect basic rules to hold when they are browsing the Internet. Things like disabling the right-click context menu or messing with the back button are just obnoxious and bad style.

11

BROWSER EVENTS

To add actual useful functionality to a web page, we need to do more than inspecting and modifying the document—we must be able to detect the user's actions and respond to them. This is done by handling events, which are the subject of this chapter.

Event Handlers

Key presses, scrolling, mouse clicks, and even mouse motion are all turned into *events* by your browser, and we can write code to *handle* them. For example, in Chapter 9, we set the onclick property of a button to do something when that button was clicked. That was an example of a simple event handler.

The way browser events work is, fundamentally, very simple. It is possible to register handlers for specific event types on specific DOM nodes. Whenever an event occurs, the handler for that event, if any, is called. For some events, such as key presses, knowing just that the event occurred is not enough information—you also want to know which key was pressed. To store such information, an *event object* is created for every event, and handlers can look at these objects.

It is important to realize that, even though events can fire at any time, no two handlers ever run at the same moment. If other JavaScript code is still running, the browser waits until it finishes before it calls the next handler. This also holds for code that is triggered in other ways, such as with setTimeout. In programmer jargon, browser JavaScript is *single-threaded*, which means there are never two "threads of control" running at the same time. This is, in most cases, a good thing. It is much harder to keep your data consistent when multiple things are happening at the same time.

An event, when not handled, can "bubble" through the DOM tree. This means that if you click, for example, a link in a paragraph, any handlers associated with the link are called first. If there are no such handlers or these handlers do not indicate that they have finished handling the event, the handlers for the paragraph—which is the parent of the link—are tried. After that, the handlers for the parent of the paragraph get a turn. Finally, if no JavaScript handlers have taken care of the event, the browser handles it itself. When the event was a click on a link, for example, the browser's response will be to follow that link.

Registering a Handler

So, as you can see, events are easy. The hard thing about them is that while all browsers support more or less the same functionality, Internet Explorer has a completely different interface for this functionality. And even among other browsers there are some differences in what is supported and how this is exposed.

There are four event-related actions one might want to take:

- Registering an event handler
- Getting the event object
- Extracting information from this object
- Signaling that an event has been handled

Unfortunately, none of these actions can be done in a uniform way across all the major browsers.

The first action, registering a handler, is most easily done by setting a property of a node corresponding to the event name, such as onclick or onkeypress. This does in fact work across browsers, but it has an important drawback—you can attach only one handler to an element. Most of the time, one is enough, but there are cases where this is a problem—especially when a program has to be able to work together with other programs (which might also be adding handlers).

Fortunately, there are also methods for registering handlers, which allow any number of them to be added. In Internet Explorer, you can add a click handler to a button with this code (assuming button holds a DOM node for a button):

```
button.attachEvent("onclick", function(){alert("Click!");});
```

On other browsers, the same thing is accomplished like this:

```
button.addEventListener("click", function(){print("Click!");}, false);
```

Note how on is left off in the second case. The third argument to addEventListener, false, indicates that the event should "bubble" through the DOM tree as normal. Giving true instead can be used to give this handler priority over the handlers "beneath" it (those registered on child nodes), but since Internet Explorer does not support this, it is rarely useful.

To make our life easier, we'll write a function that sees which model is supported and does the right thing:

```
function registerEventHandler(node, event, handler) {
  if (typeof node.addEventListener == "function")
    node.addEventListener(event, handler, false);
  else
    node.attachEvent("on" + event, handler);
}

registerEventHandler(button, "click", function(){print("Click (2)");});
```

The function first checks whether the addEventListener method is available and falls back to attachEvent when it isn't. It appends "on" to the event name in that case, since that's the form in which that function expects the event name.

Removing events works very much like adding them, but this time the methods detachEvent and removeEventListener are used. Note that to remove a handler, you need to pass the exact function you attached to it as an argument.

```
function unregisterEventHandler(node, event, handler) {
  if (typeof node.removeEventListener == "function")
    node.removeEventListener(event, handler, false);
  else
    node.detachEvent("on" + event, handler);
}
```

Event Objects

Most browsers pass the event object as an argument to the handler. Internet Explorer stores it in the top-level variable called event. When looking at JavaScript code, you will often come across something like event || window .event, which takes the local variable event or, if that is undefined, the top-level variable by that same name. For example, the following piece of code will cause the x- and y-coordinates of the mouse to be printed every time you click anywhere in the document:

```
registerEventHandler(document.body, "click", function(event) {
  event = event || window.event;
  print(event.clientX, ",", event.clientY);
});
```

Mouse-Related Event Types

When the user clicks his mouse, three separate events are generated. First
mousedown is generated at the moment the mouse button is pressed. Then,
mouseup is generated at the moment it is released. And finally, click is generated to indicate something was clicked. When this happens two times in
quick succession, a dblclick (double-click) event is also generated. Note
that it is possible for the mousedown and mouseup events to happen some time
apart—when the mouse button is held for a while. They also are not guaranteed to be fired on the same node.

When you attach an event handler to a button, for example, the fact
that it has been clicked is often all you need to know. When the handler
is attached to a node that has children, on the other hand, clicks from the
children will "bubble" up to it, and you will want to find out which child
has been clicked. For this purpose, event objects have a property called
target. . . or srcElement, depending on the browser.

Another interesting piece of information is the precise coordinates at
which the click occurred. Event objects related to the mouse contain clientX
and clientY properties, which give the x- and y-coordinates of the mouse, in
pixels, on the screen. Documents can scroll, though, so often these coordinates do not tell us much about the part of the document that the mouse is
over. Some browsers provide pageX and pageY properties for this purpose, but
others do not. Fortunately, the information about the amount of pixels the
document has been scrolled can be found in document.body.scrollLeft and
document.body.scrollTop.

It is also sometimes possible to find out which mouse button was pressed
using the which and button properties of event objects. Unfortunately, this is
very unreliable—some browsers pretend mice have only one button; others
report right-clicks as clicks during which the control key was held down, and
so on.

Obviously, writing all these checks and workarounds is not something
you want to do in every single event handler. In a moment, after we have
gotten acquainted with a few more incompatibilities, we will write a function
to "normalize" event objects to work the same across browsers.

Apart from clicks, we might also be interested in the movement of the
mouse. The mousemove event of a DOM node is fired whenever the mouse
moves while it is over that element. There are also mouseover and mouseout,
which are fired only when the mouse enters or leaves a node. For events of
this last type, the target (or srcElement) property points at the node that the
event is fired for, while the relatedTarget (or toElement or fromElement) prop-

```
```

erty gives the node that the mouse came from (for `mouseover`) or left to (for `mouseout`).

mouseover and mouseout can be tricky when they are registered on an element that has child nodes. Events fired for the child nodes will bubble up to the parent element, so you will also see a `mouseover` event when the mouse enters one of the child nodes. The `target` and `relatedTarget` properties can be used to detect (and ignore) such events, like this:

```
registerEventHandler(myParagraph, "mouseover", function(event) {
  event = event || window.event;
  if ((event.target || event.srcElement) == myParagraph)
    print("The mouse has entered my paragraph!");
});
```

Keyboard Events

Say we want to react to people pressing keys. There are, again, three events generated every time a key is pressed: `keydown`, `keyup`, and `keypress`. The first is generated when the key is pressed down, the second is generated when it is released, and the third is generated after that. In general, you should use `keydown` and `keyup` in cases where you really want to know which key was pressed, for example when you want to do something with the arrow keys. `keypress`, on the other hand, is to be used when you are interested in the character that is being typed. The reason for this is that there is often no character information in `keyup` and `keydown` events, and Internet Explorer does not generate a `keypress` event at all for special keys such as the arrow keys.

Finding out which key was pressed can be quite a challenge by itself. For `keydown` and `keyup` events, the event object will have a `keyCode` property, which contains a number. Most of the time, this code can be used to identify keys in a reasonably browser-independent way. Finding out which code corresponds to which key can be determined experimentally.

To find out whether the SHIFT, CTRL, or ALT key was held during a key or mouse event, you can look at the `shiftKey`, `ctrlKey`, and `altKey` properties of the event object. These do what you'd expect on most platforms, but for OS X (Apple) computers, some care is required, since they have somewhat different conventions. The OPTION key on those machines sets the `altKey` property, and the COMMAND key sets a separate property, `metaKey`.

For keypress events, you will want to know which character was typed. The event object will have a `charCode` property, which, if you are lucky, contains the Unicode number corresponding to the character that was typed, which can be converted to a one-character string with `String.fromCharCode`. Unfortunately, some browsers do not define this property, or define it as 0, and store the character code in the `keyCode` property instead. This code will cause a character to be printed whenever a key that produces a character is pressed:

```
registerEventHandler(document.body, "keypress", function(event) {
  event = event || window.event;
  var charCode = event.charCode || event.keyCode;
  if (charCode)
    print("Character '", String.fromCharCode(charCode), "' was typed.");
});
```

Stopping an Event

An event handler can "stop" the event it is handling and prevent further handling. There are two ways this can be done. First, you can prevent the event from bubbling up to parent nodes and the handlers defined on those, and second, you can prevent the browser from taking the standard action associated with such an event. It should be noted that browsers are free to ignore this—preventing the default behavior for the pressing of certain "hotkeys" will, on many browsers, not actually keep the browser from executing the normal effect of these keys.

On most browsers, event bubbling is stopped with the stopPropagation method of the event object, and default behavior is prevented with the preventDefault method. For Internet Explorer, this is done by setting the cancelBubble property of this object to true and the returnValue property to false, respectively.

Normalizing Event Objects

And that was the last of the long list of incompatibilities that we will discuss in this chapter. This means we can finally write the event normalizer function and move on to more interesting things.

The following function goes over all the event object properties we discussed before and makes sure each one can be found under a standard name. A stop method is added, which cancels both the bubbling and the default action of the event. Some browsers already provide this, in which case we leave it as it is.

```
function normalizeEvent(event) {
  if (!event.stopPropagation) {
    event.stopPropagation = function() {this.cancelBubble = true;};
    event.preventDefault = function() {this.returnValue = false;};
  }
  if (!event.stop)
    event.stop = function() {
      this.stopPropagation();
      this.preventDefault();
    };

  if (event.srcElement && !event.target)
    event.target = event.srcElement;
```

```
  if ((event.toElement || event.fromElement) && !event.relatedTarget)
    event.relatedTarget = event.toElement || event.fromElement;
  if (event.clientX != undefined && event.pageX == undefined) {
    event.pageX = event.clientX + document.body.scrollLeft;
    event.pageY = event.clientY + document.body.scrollTop;
  }
  if (event.type == "keypress")
    event.character = String.fromCharCode(event.charCode || event.keyCode);
  return event;
}
```

Having this function, we can write more convenient wrappers for
registerEventHandler and unregisterEventHandler:

```
function addHandler(node, type, handler) {
  function wrapHandler(event) {
    handler(normalizeEvent(event || window.event));
  }
  registerEventHandler(node, type, wrapHandler);
  return {node: node, type: type, handler: wrapHandler};
}

function removeHandler(object) {
  unregisterEventHandler(object.node, object.type, object.handler);
}
```

The addHandler function returns an object that can be used to remove
the handler again. The inner function takes care of finding the event object
for us. It could be used like this, where we add a handler to a text field that
prevents the user from typing the letter Q:

```
var blockQ = addHandler(textfield, "keypress", function(event) {
  if (event.character.toLowerCase() == "q")
    event.stop();
});

// Later...
removeHandler(blockQ);
```

Tracking Focus

Other event types that can be useful are focus and blur, which are fired on
elements that can be "focused," such as form inputs. focus, obviously, happens when you put the focus on the element, for example by clicking it.
blur is JavaScript-speak for "unfocus" and is fired when the focus leaves the
element.

The following code would cause the background of a text input field to be yellow as long as it is focused:

```
addHandler(textfield, "focus", function(event) {
  event.target.style.backgroundColor = "yellow";
});
addHandler(textfield, "blur", function(event) {
  event.target.style.backgroundColor = "";
});
```

Form Events

Each changeable form element is capable of firing change events. These are fired when the content or value of the input has changed. Note that for some inputs, such as text inputs, it does not fire until the element is unfocused. This code will print a message every time the content of a text field is changed:

```
addHandler(textfield, "change", function(event) {
  print("Content of text field changed to '", event.target.value, "'.");
});
```

Forms also have a submit event, which is fired when they submit. It can be stopped to prevent the submit from taking place. This gives us a *much* better way to do the form validation we saw in the previous chapter. You just register a submit handler, which stops the event when the content of the form is not valid. That way, when the user does not have JavaScript enabled, the form will still work; it just won't have instant validation.

Window Events

Some events are fired on the window object as a whole, rather than on individual DOM nodes. For example, the load event on a window fires when the document is fully loaded, which can be useful if your script needs to do some kind of initialization that has to wait until the whole document is present.

Most of the time it is best to leave the laying out of a document to the browser, but there are effects that can be produced only by having a piece of JavaScript set the exact sizes of some nodes in a document. When you do this, make sure you also listen for resize events on the window, which is fired every time the size of the window changes, and recalculate the sizes of your element every time the window is resized. Whenever the document is scrolled, the browser fires a scroll event on the window object.

Example: Implementing Sokoban

Armed with addHandler and the dom function from the previous chapter, we are ready for more challenging feats of document manipulation. As an exercise, we will implement the game known as *Sokoban*. This is something of a classic, but you may not have seen it before. The rules are these: There is a grid made up of walls, empty space, and one or more "exits." On this grid, there are a number of crates or stones, and a little dude that the player controls. This dude can be moved horizontally and vertically into empty squares and can push the boulders around, provided that there is empty space behind them. The goal of the game is to move a given number of boulders into the exits. It looks something like this:

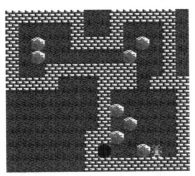

Level Input Format

Just like the terraria from Chapter 6, a Sokoban level can be represented as text. Assume we have an array of level objects. Each level has a property field, containing a textual representation of the level, and a property boulders, indicating the amount of boulders that must be expelled to finish the level. The level depicted in the screenshot looks like this:

```
var level = {boulders: 10,
             field: ["#####  ##### ",
                     "#    # #   # ",
                     "# O  #### O # ",
                     "# O @    O # ",
                     "# #######O # ",
                     "####   ### ###",
                     "       #    #",
                     "       #O    #",
                     "       # O   #",
                     "       ## O  #",
                     "       #*O O  #",
                     "       ########"]};
```

The # characters are walls, the spaces are empty squares, the 0 characters are used for boulders, an at sign (@) is for the starting location of the player, and an asterisk (*) is for the exit.

Program Design

Our game will use this textual representation only to store level layouts. While playing, we want it to look like the picture we saw earlier. If we have five images, showing an empty field (empty.png), an empty field with the player on it (player.png), a boulder (boulder.png), a wall (wall.png), and an exit hole (exit.png), we can use these to build up the game board.

The whole board will be held in a div element, which then contains an image (img element) for every square of the board. At the end of each row, we need a br element—a "break" that serves much the same purpose as a newline character in normal text—to make the next image appear on the next "line."

It would be possible to use this DOM structure as the main representation of our data—when we want to see whether there is a wall in a given square, we just find the right image element and look at its src property. For simpler things, this approach can be good enough, but it is somewhat messy and slow, so I chose to keep a separate data structure representing the state of the playing field.

This data structure is a two-dimensional grid of objects, representing the squares of the playing field. Each of the objects must store its current content (as a string). It should also contain a reference to the image element that is used to display it in the document, because it is responsible for updating this image's src property when its content changes.

That gives us two kinds of objects—one to hold the grid of the playing field and one to represent the individual cells in this grid. If we want the game to also do things such as move to the next level at the appropriate moment and be able to reset the current level when you mess up, we can add a third object, the "controller," which creates or removes the field objects at the appropriate moment.

Game Board Representation

Let's start with the objects representing the squares on the game's field. They consist only of a constructor and a single, simple method:

```
function Square(character, img) {
  this.img = img;
  var content = {"@": "player", "#": "wall", "*": "exit",
                 " ": "empty", "0": "boulder"}[character];
  if (content == null)
    throw new Error("Unrecognized character: '" + character + "'");
  this.setContent(content);
}
```

```
Square.prototype.setContent = function(content) {
  this.content = content;
  this.img.src = "img/sokoban/" + content + ".png";
}
```

Because the field is created from a string, the Square constructor has to know how to convert a character in this string to a meaningful name (which is also the name of the image that should be shown for the square). To do this, it uses an object whose property names are characters and whose property values are names.

The setContent method updates both the square's content property (which should be a string like "boulder") and the src property of the square's image element.

The next object type, which represents the whole playing field, will be called SokobanField. Its constructor is given a level object; it is responsible for building the DOM structure for this level and a grid (an array of arrays) of Square objects.

To identify the individual squares, and to indicate directions, we will again use the Point object type from Chapter 6, which had x and y properties, and an add method that allows two points to be added together. In this constructor, such a point object is created to remember the player position.

```
function SokobanField(level) {
  this.fieldDiv = dom("DIV");
  this.squares = [];
  this.bouldersToGo = level.boulders;

  for (var y = 0; y < level.field.length; y++) {
    var line = level.field[y], squareRow = [];
    for (var x = 0; x < line.length; x++) {
      var img = dom("IMG");
      this.fieldDiv.appendChild(img);
      squareRow.push(new Square(line.charAt(x), img));
      if (line.charAt(x) == "@")
        this.playerPos = new Point(x, y);
    }
    this.fieldDiv.appendChild(dom("BR"));
    this.squares.push(squareRow);
  }
}
```

To make it easy for the game code to report the amount of boulders the player still has to push out of the field and to find out whether the level has been completed, the field object provides two simple methods:

```
SokobanField.prototype.status = function() {
  return this.bouldersToGo + " boulder" +
    (this.bouldersToGo == 1 ? "" : "s") + " to go.";
```

```
};
SokobanField.prototype.won = function() {
  return this.bouldersToGo <= 0;
};
```

Of course, we will also need methods for inserting the field into the DOM tree. We could just reach in and use the `fieldDiv` property of the field object, but it is cleaner to provide an interface for this:

```
SokobanField.prototype.place = function(where) {
  where.appendChild(this.fieldDiv);
};
SokobanField.prototype.remove = function() {
  this.fieldDiv.parentNode.removeChild(this.fieldDiv);
};
```

The `SokobanField` object will also take care of moving the player and boulders around through a `move` method that is given a `Point` argument indicating which direction the player wants to move—for example, `-1`, `0` to move left.

This method proceeds in two steps. If there is a boulder in the player's way, it sees whether this boulder can be pushed (either into an empty square or into an exit). After that, if the square in front of the player is empty—which is also the case if a boulder was just moved out of there—the player is moved into it.

When a boulder is dropped into the exit, the `bouldersToGo` property is updated so that the status and `won` methods will return up-to-date information.

```
SokobanField.prototype.move = function(direction) {
  var playerSquare = this.squares[this.playerPos.y][this.playerPos.x],
      targetPos = this.playerPos.add(direction),
      targetSquare = this.squares[targetPos.y][targetPos.x];

  // First, see if the player can push a boulder...
  if (targetSquare.content == "boulder") {
    var pushPos = targetPos.add(direction),
        pushSquare = this.squares[pushPos.y][pushPos.x];
    if (pushSquare.content == "empty") {
      targetSquare.setContent("empty");
      pushSquare.setContent("boulder");
    }
    else if (pushSquare.content == "exit") {
      targetSquare.setContent("empty");
      this.bouldersToGo--;
    }
  }
```

```
  // Then, try to move...
  if (targetSquare.content == "empty") {
    playerSquare.setContent("empty");
    targetSquare.setContent("player");
    this.playerPos = targetPos;
  }
};
```

With what we have now, we could run the following code and see the field appear:

```
(new SokobanField(level)).place(document.body);
```

This field is still completely noninteractive. Next up, we write a controller object to remedy that and make the game playable.

The Controller Object

The controller will be an object type called SokobanGame, which is responsible for the following functions:

- Preparing a place where the game field can be placed

- Building and removing SokobanField objects

- Capturing key events and calling the move method on current field with the correct argument

- Keeping track of the current level number and moving to the next level when a level is won

- Adding buttons to reset the current level or the whole game (back to level 0)

We start with a constructor. It takes an array of level objects as its first argument, which it will allow the player to play through. The second argument should be a DOM node to which it should append the game interface. It builds a simple set of DOM nodes to wrap around the playing field, consisting of two buttons and a div element to display status information.

The click event handlers on the buttons are simply attached to methods of the game object (the method function was defined in Chapter 6) that handle the action associated with these buttons. We will define these in a moment. The keydown handler is attached to the whole document, meaning all keydown events that are not handled by some other handler end up being handled by the game.

```
function SokobanGame(levels, place) {
  this.levels = levels;
  var newGame = dom("BUTTON", null, "New game");
```

```
addHandler(newGame, "click", method(this, "newGame"));
var reset = dom("BUTTON", null, "Reset level");
addHandler(reset, "click", method(this, "resetLevel"));
this.status = dom("DIV");
this.container = dom("DIV", null, dom("H1", null, "Sokoban"),
                  dom("DIV", null, newGame, " ", reset), this.status);
place.appendChild(this.container);
addHandler(document, "keydown", method(this, "keyDown"));
this.newGame();
}
```

The newGame function does very little work itself; it just sets the game's
level property to zero and lets resetLevel set up the level. This is the method
responsible for creating and showing the playing field. If there was already a
field present, this is first removed.

```
SokobanGame.prototype.newGame = function() {
  this.level = 0;
  this.resetLevel();
};
SokobanGame.prototype.resetLevel = function() {
  if (this.field)
    this.field.remove();
  this.field = new SokobanField(this.levels[this.level]);
  this.field.place(this.container);
  this.updateStatus();
};
SokobanGame.prototype.updateStatus = function() {
  this.status.innerHTML = "Level " + (1 + this.level) + ": " +
    this.field.status();
};
```

The only thing left to do now is define the keyDown method, which will
cause the game character to move when the user presses the arrow keys.

The method uses an object to map key codes to Point objects representing a direction in which to move. Only events whose keyCode property
is found in this object are handled.

The direction Point is handed off to the move method of the field object.
This might result in the status to change, so afterward updateStatus is called
to update the status text, and we check whether the player has won the game
yet.

If the game is won and there are more levels after this one, it moves to
the next level. If not, it congratulates the player on winning and restarts the
game.

```
var arrowKeyCodes = {
  37: new Point(-1, 0), // left
  38: new Point(0, -1), // up
  39: new Point(1, 0),  // right
  40: new Point(0, 1)   // down
};

SokobanGame.prototype.keyDown = function(event) {
  if (arrowKeyCodes.hasOwnProperty(event.keyCode)) {
    event.stop();
    this.field.move(arrowKeyCodes[event.keyCode]);
    this.updateStatus();
    if (this.field.won()) {
      if (this.level < this.levels.length - 1) {
        alert("Excellent! Going to the next level.");
        this.level++;
        this.resetLevel();
      }
      else {
        alert("You win! Game over.");
        this.newGame();
      }
    }
  }
};
```

12

HTTP REQUESTS

As mentioned in Chapter 9, communication on the World Wide Web happens over the *HTTP protocol.* This chapter describes how to use this protocol to make your client-side program talk to your web server.

The HTTP Protocol

A simple HTTP request might look like this:

```
GET /files/data.txt HTTP/1.1
Host: eloquentjavascript.net
User-Agent: My Imaginary Browser
```

This asks for the file files/data.txt from the server at eloquentjavascript .net. In addition, it specifies that this request uses version 1.1 of the HTTP protocol—version 1.0 is also still in use and works slightly differently. The Host and User-Agent lines are called *headers.* These follow a pattern: They start with a word that identifies the information they contain, followed by a colon, and then the actual information. The User-Agent header tells the server which program is being used to make the request. Other kinds of headers are often sent along, for example to state the types of documents that the client can understand or the language that it prefers.

When given the previous request, the server might send the following response:

```
HTTP/1.1 200 OK
Last-Modified: Mon, 23 Jul 2007 08:41:56 GMT
Content-Length: 40
Content-Type: text/plain

This is the content of the file data.txt
```

The first line indicates again the version of the HTTP protocol, followed by the status of the request. In this case the status code is 200, meaning "OK, nothing out of the ordinary happened, I am sending you the file." This is followed by a few headers, indicating (in this case) the last time the file was modified, its length, and its type (plain text). After the headers, you get a blank line, followed by the file itself. This is called the response *body*.

Apart from requests starting with *GET*, which indicates the client just wants to fetch a document, the word *POST* can also be used to indicate that a body will be sent along with the request. The difference between these *methods* (which is what the verb at the start of a request is called) was shortly touched on Chapter 9, when discussing forms. There are other types of requests, for example *PUT* to put a document onto the server and *DELETE* to delete a document. These are less widely used, mostly because browsers do not provide an easy way to issue them—GET is used for every link you follow, POST is used for forms that have method="post" specified, but no corresponding conventions exist for PUT and DELETE.

The XMLHttpRequest API

When you click a link, submit a form, or in some other way encourage your browser to go to a new page, it will make an HTTP request and, if successful, show the newly loaded document. In typical situations, this is just what you want—it is how the Web traditionally works. Sometimes, however, a JavaScript program wants to communicate with the server without reloading the page.

To be able to do something like that, the program must make the HTTP request itself. Contemporary browsers provide an interface for doing this. As with opening new windows, this interface is subject to some restrictions—to prevent a script from doing anything scary, it is allowed to make HTTP requests only to the domain that the current page came from, meaning a page on *http://www.evil.org/* cannot cause your browser to fetch a page from *http://www.yourbank.com/*, since you might be logged in there, and such a request could instruct the bank to transfer your money to, say, the owner of *http://www.evil.org/*.

Creating a Request Object

An object used to make an HTTP request can, on most browsers, be created by simply doing new XMLHttpRequest(). Internet Explorer 6, which is still being used by a few recalcitrants, requires you to do new ActiveXObject("Msxml2 .XMLHTTP") instead. We are already used to writing incompatibility wrappers by now, so here we go again:

```
function requestObject() {
  if (window.XMLHttpRequest)
    return new XMLHttpRequest();
  else if (window.ActiveXObject)
    return new ActiveXObject("Msxml2.XMLHTTP");
  else
    throw new Error("Could not create HTTP request object.");
}
```

This function sees whether the modern method is supported, falls back to the Internet Explorer 6 method if not, and throws an error if that doesn't work either.

Simple Requests

Now that we have our request object, we can use it to make a request similar to the example shown earlier:

```
var request = requestObject();
request.open("GET", "files/data.txt", false);
request.send(null);

request.responseText;
→ "This is the content of the file data.txt"
```

The open method is used to configure a request. In this case, we choose to make a GET request for our data.txt file. The URL given here is relative—it does not contain the http:// part or a server name, which means it will look for the file on the server that the current document came from. The third parameter, false, will be discussed in a moment. After open has been called, the actual request can be made with the send method. When the request is a POST request, the data to be sent to the server (as a string) can be passed to this method. For GET requests, just pass null.

After the request has been made, the responseText property of the request object contains the content of the retrieved document. The headers that the server sent back can be inspected with the getResponseHeader and getAllResponseHeaders functions. The first looks up a specific header, and the second gives us a string containing all the headers. These can occasionally be useful to get some extra information about the document.

```
request.getResponseHeader("Content-Type");
→ "text/plain"
```

If you want to add headers to the request that is sent to the server, for example to provide authentication information or to tell the server what kind of response you want back (read a book on HTTP to find out how), you can do so with the setRequestHeader method. This takes two strings as arguments: the name and the value of the header.

The response code, which was 200 in the example, can be found under the status property. If something goes wrong, this cryptic code will indicate it. For example, 404 means the file you asked for did not exist. The statusText contains a slightly less cryptic description of the status:

```
request.status;
→ 200
request.statusText;
→ "OK"
```

When you want to check whether a request succeeded, comparing the status to 200 is usually enough. However, more complicated web services might also use different success codes—for example 204, which means "no content," indicating the server successfully received the request but doesn't have anything to say in response.

Making Asynchronous Requests

When a request is made as in the example shown earlier, the call to the send method does not return until the request is finished. This is convenient, because it means the responseText is available after the call to send, and we can start using it immediately. There is a problem, though: When the server is slow or the file is big, doing a request might take quite a while. As long as this is happening, the program is waiting, which causes the whole browser to wait. Until the request finishes, the user cannot do anything. Pages that run on a local network, which is fast and reliable, might get away with doing requests like this. Pages on the great, big, unreliable Internet should not.

When the third argument to open is true, the request is set to be *asynchronous*. This means that send will return right away, while the request happens in the background.

```
request.open("GET", "files/data.txt", true);
request.send(null);
```

After this, the program will continue running while the request happens in the background. If you look at the responseText property right after calling send, it'll be null. If you look again after a few seconds, the request will have completed, and the property has been filled in.

"Waiting a few seconds" could be implemented with `setTimeout` or something like that, but there is a better way. A request object has a `readyState` property, indicating the state it is in. To react to changes in this status, you can set the `onreadystatechange` property of the object to a function. This function will be called every time the state changes.

A request object will start in state 0. Once you call `open` on it, it goes to 1. Then, calling `send` puts the object in state 2. When it starts reading a response, it goes to 3, and finally, when the whole response was read, the request reaches state 4. 4 is usually the only state we are really interested in, since that is the state that indicates the request has finished. This code waits, asynchronously, for our request to finish and then prints out the status code and text:

```
request.open("GET", "files/data.txt", true);
request.onreadystatechange = function() {
  if (request.readyState == 4)
    print(request.status + " " + request.statusText);
};
request.send(null);
```

Fetching XML Data

So, why is the request object called an *XML* HTTP request? This is a bit of a misleading name. *XML* is a way to store textual data. It uses tags and attributes like HTML but is more structured and flexible—to store your own kinds of data, you may define your own types of XML tags. These HTTP request objects have some built-in functionality for dealing with retrieved XML documents, which is why they have XML in their name. They can also handle other types of documents, though, so `HttpRequest` would have been a more sensible name.

When the file retrieved by the request object is an XML document, the request's `responseXML` property will hold a representation of this document. This representation works like the DOM objects discussed in Chapter 10, except that it doesn't have HTML-specific functionality, such as `style` or `innerHTML`. `responseXML` gives us a document object, whose `documentElement` property refers to the outer tag of the XML document. Say we have this document (`files/fruit.xml`):

```
<fruits>
  <fruit name="banana" color="yellow"/>
  <fruit name="lemon" color="yellow"/>
  <fruit name="cherry" color="red"/>
</fruits>
```

We could retrieve it like this:

```
request.open("GET", "files/fruit.xml", false);
request.send(null);
request.responseXML.documentElement.childNodes.length;
→ 3
```

XML documents can be used to exchange structured information with the server. Their form—tags contained inside other tags—is often very suitable to store things that would be tricky to represent as simple flat text. The DOM interface is rather clumsy for extracting information, though, and XML documents are somewhat wordy.

Reading JSON Data

As an alternative to XML, JavaScript programmers have come up with something called *JavaScript Object Notation* (JSON). This uses the syntax of Java-Script values to represent structured information in a more minimalist way. A JSON document is a file containing a single JavaScript object or array, which in turn contains any number of other objects, arrays, strings, numbers, Booleans, or `null` values. For an example, this is what `fruit.json` could look like:

```
{"banana": "yellow",
 "lemon":  "yellow",
 "cherry": "red"}
```

Such a piece of text can be converted to a regular JavaScript value by using the eval function. eval *evaluates* the text it is given as a JavaScript program. eval("1+1"), for example, will produce 2. In this case, we want to evaluate the array in the JSON document so that it becomes an actual array object.

Before passing a JSON document to eval, you should wrap it in parentheses, because when a program starts with a { character, that character will be interpreted as the start of a block of code, not as the start of an object. This program fetches the fruit data and looks up the color of lemons:

```
request.open("GET", "files/fruit.json", true);
request.onreadystatechange = function() {
  if (request.readyState == 4) {
    var data = eval("(" + request.responseText + ")");
    print(data["lemon"]);
  }
};
request.send(null);
```

When running eval on a piece of text, you have to keep in mind that this means you let the piece of text run whichever code it wants. Since JavaScript only allows us to make requests to our own domain, you will usually know exactly what kind of text you are getting, and this is not a problem. In situations where you do not have control over the text, calling eval is not recommended—you might put your system, or the users of your site, at risk.

A Basic Request Wrapper

When making lots of requests, we do not want to repeat the whole open, send, onreadystatechange ritual every time. A very simple wrapper could look like this:

```
function simpleHttpRequest(url, success, failure) {
  var request = requestObject();
  request.open("GET", url, true);
  request.onreadystatechange = function() {
    if (request.readyState == 4) {
      if (request.status == 200 || !failure)
        success(request.responseText);
      else if (failure)
        failure(request.status, request.statusText);
    }
  };
  request.send(null);
}
```

The function retrieves the URL it is given and calls the function it is given as a second argument with the content. When a third argument is given, this is used to indicate failure—a non-200 status code.

To be able to do more complex requests, the function could be made to accept extra parameters to specify the method (GET or POST), an optional string to post as data, a way to add extra headers, and so on. With so many arguments, the function should probably use an argument-object as shown in Chapter 7.

Learning HTTP

HTTP is a very clever and flexible protocol. Whenever you find yourself making serious use of it, and *especially* if you end up designing an HTTP interface (which comes up in almost all server-side web programming), I want you to promise me that you will first study the way the protocol actually works.

The reason I ask is that most programmers start working with HTTP with only a very minimal understanding of it. I certainly did. They don't know how to properly take advantage, or even deal with, features such as caching (a mechanism to prevent repeatedly fetching the same document) and Internet media types (a way to identify the format of documents), and the result is that they build overcomplicated, brittle, wrong-headed wrappers in an attempt to "hide" the use of HTTP. When used correctly, HTTP is a great match for most forms of communication and does not need to be hidden.

There are various books and Internet resources available to help "get" HTTP. As usual, be wary of the advice offered on Internet forums and websites with poor spelling, since people who know a little still tend to talk a lot. For the technically minded, the HTTP standard is actually a very good and enlightening read, but, like most standard documents, it is rather dense. A more forgiving read is Gourley and Totty's *HTTP: The Definitive Guide*, published by O'Reilly.

INDEX

Symbols

&&, as logical and operator, 14, 28
* (asterisk), as multiplication
    operator, 11, 27, 142
*= operator, 23
\ (backslash), 12, 140, 141
{} (braces)
    for blocks, 21, 32, 194
    for objects, 43, 96
= (equal sign), 15, 43, 44
==, as equal to operator, 14, 26,
    46, 55
===, as precisely equal to operator, 26
! (exclamation mark), as not
    operator, 14
!=, as not equal to operator, 14
!==, as not precisely equal to
    operator, 26
/ (forward slash), as division
    operator, 11, 27
/= operator, 23
> (greater-than sign), 13
>=, as greater than or equal to
    operator, 14
< (less-than sign), 13
<=, as less than or equal to
    operator, 14
- (minus sign), 11, 13, 27
-= operator, 23
-- operator, 23
() parentheses
    for applying functions, 17, 33–34
    for grouping, 11, 142

% (percent sign), as modulo
    operator, 11, 23
+ (plus sign), 11, 12, 27, 142
++ operator, 23
+= operator, 23
?: operator, 76
" (quotation marks), 12, 44, 87, 140
; (semicolon), 15, 23
[] (square brackets)
    for accessing properties, 43,
        44, 47
    for arrays, 46, 47
    in regular expressions, 140
||, as logical or operator, 14, 28, 39

A

a (HTML tag), 86, 89
absolute positioning, 171
abstraction, 5, 36, 71, 102
acos function, 61
addEventListener method, 175
addHandler function, 179
alert function, 17, 35
algorithm, 46, 74
altKey property, 177
anonymous function, 34, 73, 133
appendChild method, 167
application
    of functions, 17, 33, 35, 37
    of operators, 11
apply method, 75, 94, 108
argument, 17, 30, 35, 86, 136
arguments object, 59, 75, 91

HTML(HyperText Markup Language), 7, 77–78, 152
  attribute, 78
  generation, 81, 86
  styling, 169
  tag, 77
  whitespace rules, 169
HTTP (HyperText Transfer Protocol), 151, 189–190, 195
  header, 189, 191
  method, 158, 190, 191
  request, 152, 156, 189
  response, 190
  status code, 192, 195
HyperText Markup Language. *See* HTML (HyperText Markup Language)
HyperText Transfer Protocol. *See* HTTP (HyperText Transfer Protocol)

I

i variable, 47
id attribute, 166, 169
if keyword, 19, 26, 76
image, 182
img (HTML tag), 78, 165, 166
in operator, 44, 52, 98, 100
indentation, 22, 49
indexOf method, 51, 83
infinite loop, 69
inherit method, 123
inheritance, 115–116, 122, 125–128
.ini file example, 147–149
inner function, 31, 54, 56
innerHTML property, 165
input (HTML tag), 157, 159
insertBefore method, 168
instanceof operator, 126
interface, 94, 101, 106, 110, 130
  design, 36, 37, 53, 102, 134
    composability, 135
    layering, 135
  object, 134

invalid input, 63
invoking functions, 17, 33, 35, 37
isA method, 126
isImage function, 165
isNaN function, 19, 27
isTextNode function, 165

J

Java, 6
JavaScript, 6
  availability of, 2, 162
  console, 68
  flexibility of, 6
  syntax, 14
  trying out, 7
  versions of, 6
  weaknesses of, 6, 100, 130
JavaScript Object Notation (JSON), 194–195
join method, 48, 88
jQuery, 137
JSON (JavaScript Object Notation), 194–195

K

keyCode property, 177
keydown event, 177, 185
keypress event, 177
keyup event, 177
keyword, 16

L

lastChild property, 164, 166
lastElement function, 65, 66
left style, 171
length property, 43, 46, 59, 62
less-than (<) operator, 13
less than or equal to (<=) operator, 13
lexical scoping, 31–32, 73, 91
library, 137
Lichen type, 118
LichenEater type, 119

relatedTarget property, 176
relative URL, 157
removeChild method, 168
removeEventListener method, 175
removeHandler function, 179
renderFile function, 90
renderHTML function, 88
repetition, avoiding of, 36, 116, 126
replace method, 87, 144
replaceChild method, 168
requestObject function, 191
reserved words, 16
resize event, 180
response body, 190
responseText property, 191
responseXML property, 193
return keyword, 30, 31, 58, 95
return value, 17, 30
returnValue property, 178
round function, 37, 61
run-time error, 63, 64

S

sandboxing, 153, 154, 190
scientific notation, 10
script (HTML tag), 7, 131, 154
scroll event, 180
scrollLeft property, 176
scrollTop property, 176
search method, 139
security, 153, 154, 194
select (HTML tag), 157
self variable, 108, 117
semicolon (;), 14, 23
send method, 191, 192
server, 151
set (data structure), 45
setAttribute method, 167
setDate method, 55
setFullYear method, 55
setHours method, 55
setInterval method, 156
setMinutes method, 55
setMonth method, 55
setRequestHeader method, 192
setSeconds method, 55

setTimeout method, 155
shiftKey property, 177
shortcut evaluation, 28, 39
side effect, 15, 17, 37, 45, 53, 84
simpleHttpRequest function, 195
simulation, 102, 109, 115, 120
sin function, 61
slice method, 50
Sokoban, 181–187
    levels, 181–182
    SokobanField type, 183
    SokobanGame type, 185
spellcheck example, 135
spinning node example, 171
split method, 49, 82
sqrt function, 61
square brackets, [ ]
    for accessing properties, 43,
        44, 47
    for arrays, 46, 47
    in regular expressions, 140
square function, 29
square root, 61
Square type, 182
src property, 166, 182
srcElement property, 176
stack, 33
    overflow, 33, 38
    unwinding of, 66
standard environment, 17
startsWith function, 50
state, 15, 21–23
statement, 14, 21
status property, 192
statusText property, 192
stop method, 178
stopPropagation method, 178
String function, 19, 37
String type, 12, 48
Stroustrup, Bjarne, 78
StupidBug type, 106
style property, 170
style sheets, 169–172
submit event, 180
submit method, 159
subtype, 123
sum function, 61, 73, 75, 92

sup (HTML tag), 89
supertype, 123
switch keyword, 24

T

tag function, 86
tan function, 61
target property, 176
tentacle (variable analogy), 16, 25
ternary operator, 76
terrarium, 102–122
    action object, 106
    bug object, 106
    Terrarium type, 106
test method, 141
testing, automated, 70
text adventure example, 125–128
text input, 18, 157
text node, 164
    content of, 165
    distinguishing, 165
textual data, 12
this variable, 94, 95, 108
threading, 174, 192
throw keyword, 66, 67
time zone, 56
timer, 155
toLowerCase method, 48
top style, 171
top-level variable, 31, 131
toString method, 62, 96, 103, 107,
        111, 114
toUpperCase method, 48
trigonometry, 61, 171
true, 13
try keyword, 67, 68
type, 9, 13
    checking, 64
    conversion, 26, 27
typeof operator, 13

U

unary operator, 13
undefined value, 25, 30, 31, 35, 43
unhandled exception, 68
Unicode, 13, 177

Universal Resource Locators
        (URLs), 152, 156, 191
unregisterEventHandler function, 175
unwinding the stack, 66
URLs (Universal Resource
        Locators), 152, 156, 191

V

value, 9
value property, 159
var keyword, 15, 31
variable, 4, 15, 21, 30. *See also*
        global variable
    model of, 16
    naming, 15, 16
    scope, 31, 34, 108
variadic function, 60

W

Web, the, 6, 151–153, 189
Web browser, 2, 7, 190
    detection, 161
    events, 173–187
    incompatibility, 160, 166
Weizenbaum, Joseph, 2
which property, 176
while loop, 5, 20, 26
width style, 172
wiki syntax, 79
window object, 132, 153
World Wide Web (WWW), 6,
        151–153, 189
write method, 154

X

XML (eXtensible Markup Lan-
        guage), 193
XMLHttpRequest type, 191, 193

Y

Yahoo! User Interface (YUI), 137

Z

zeroPad function, 37

UPDATES

Visit *http://www.nostarch.com/ejs.htm* for updates, errata, and other information.

COLOPHON

The fonts used in *Eloquent JavaScript* are New Baskerville, Futura, The Sans Mono Condensed and Dogma. The book was typeset with LaTeX 2_ε package nostarch by Boris Veytsman *(2008/06/06 v1.3 Typesetting books for No Starch Press)*.

This book was printed on demand at Lightning Source Incorporated in La Vergne, Tennessee.

The Electronic Frontier Foundation (EFF) is the leading organization defending civil liberties in the digital world. We defend free speech on the Internet, fight illegal surveillance, promote the rights of innovators to develop new digital technologies, and work to ensure that the rights and freedoms we enjoy are enhanced — rather than eroded — as our use of technology grows.

EFF.ORG

ELECTRONIC FRONTIER FOUNDATION

Protecting Rights and Promoting Freedom on the Electronic Frontier

LAND OF LISP

Learn to Program in Lisp, One Game at a Time!

by CONRAD BARSKI, M.D.

Lisp is a uniquely powerful programming language that, despite its academic reputation, is actually very practical. *Land of Lisp* brings the language into the real world, teaching readers Lisp by showing them how to write several complete Lisp-based games, including a text adventure, an evolution simulation, and a robot battle. While building these games, readers learn the core concepts of Lisp programming, such as recursion, input/output, object-oriented programming, and macros. And thanks to Lisp's powerful syntax, the example code is short and easy to understand. The book is filled with the author's brilliant Lisp cartoons, which are sure to appeal to many Lisp fans and, in the tradition of all No Starch Press titles, make learning more fun.

OCTOBER 2010, 504 PP., $49.95
ISBN 978-1-59327-281-4

GRAY HAT PYTHON

Python Programming for Hackers and Reverse Engineers

by JUSTIN SEITZ

Gray Hat Python explains how to complete various hacking tasks with Python, which is fast becoming the programming language of choice for hackers, reverse engineers, and software testers. Author Justin Seitz explains the concepts behind hacking tools like debuggers, Trojans, fuzzers, and emulators. He then goes on to explain how to harness existing Python-based security tools and build new ones when the pre-built ones just won't cut it. The book teaches readers how to automate tedious reversing and security tasks; sniff secure traffic out of an encrypted web browser session; use PyDBG, Immunity Debugger, Sulley, IDAPython, and PyEMU; and more.

APRIL 2009, 216 PP., $39.95
ISBN 978-1-59327-192-3

LEARN YOU A HASKELL FOR GREAT GOOD!

by MIRAN LIPOVAČA

Learn You a Haskell for Great Good! is a fun, illustrated guide to learning Haskell, a functional programming language that's growing in popularity. The book introduces programmers familiar with imperative languages (such as C++, Java, or Python) to the unique aspects of functional programming. Packed with jokes, pop culture references, and the author's own hilarious artwork, *Learn You a Haskell for Great Good!* eases the learning curve of this complex language and is a perfect starting point for any programmer looking to expand their horizons.

MARCH 2011, 400 PP., $44.95
ISBN 978-1-59327-283-8

MAP SCRIPTING 101
An Example-Driven Guide to Building Interactive Maps with Bing, Yahoo!, and Google Maps

by ADAM DUVANDER

Map Scripting 101 uses a project-based approach to teach readers how to create useful and fun online map mashups like weather maps and local concert trackers. Author Adam DuVander shows readers how to use Mapstraction, an open source JavaScript library, to create and manipulate basic maps by setting zoom levels, showing and hiding markers, geocoding addresses, customizing maps for visitors based on their locales, and so on. Readers will also learn to handle complex GIS (geographic information system) data and formats like KML and GeoRSS, and to create graphical overlays to make sense of data and trends. This book is perfect for any web developer, whether their goal is to build a map to track earthquakes around the world or to simply mark the best coffee shops in town.

AUGUST 2010, 376 PP., $34.95
ISBN 978-1-59327-271-5

WICKED COOL PHP
Real-World Scripts That Solve Difficult Problems

by WILLIAM STEINMETZ *with* BRIAN WARD

Rather than focus on the basics of the language, *Wicked Cool PHP* provides (and explains) PHP scripts that can be implemented immediately to simplify webmasters' lives. These include a wide variety of scripts that process credit cards, check for valid email addresses, template HTML, override PHP's default settings, and serve dynamic images and text. Readers will also find extensive sections on working with forms, words, and files; ways to harden PHP by closing common security holes; and instructions for keeping data and transactions secure. By exploring working code, readers learn how to customize their web server's behavior, prevent spammers from adding annoying comments, scrape information from other websites, and much more.

FEBRUARY 2008, 216 PP., $29.95
ISBN 978-1-59327-173-2

PHONE:
800.420.7240 OR
415.863.9900
MONDAY THROUGH FRIDAY,
9 A.M. TO 5 P.M. (PST)

FAX:
415.863.9950
24 HOURS A DAY,
7 DAYS A WEEK

EMAIL:
SALES@NOSTARCH.COM

WEB:
WWW.NOSTARCH.COM

MAIL:
NO STARCH PRESS
245 8th STREET
SAN FRANCISCO, CA 94103
USA

CPSIA information can be obtained at www.ICGtesting.com
Printed in the USA
BVOW09s0341050814

361697BV00015B/71/P